Terry Johnson

Dead Funny

Methuen Drama

Methuen Modern Plays

First published in Great Britain 1994
by Methuen Drama
an imprint of Reed Consumer Books Ltd
Michelin House, 81 Fulham Road, London SW3 6RB
and Auckland, Melbourne, Singapore and Toronto
and distributed in the United States of America
by Heinemann, a division of Reed Publishing (USA) Inc
361 Hanover Street, Portsmouth, New Hampshire NH 03801 5959

Reprinted 1994

ISBN 0-413-68340-0

A CIP catalogue record for this book
is available from the British Library.

Typeset by Wilmaset Ltd, Birkenhead, Wirral

Printed and bound in Great Britain by
Cox & Wyman Ltd, Reading, Berkshire

Characters

Eleanor   Thirty-nine. Attractive, middle-class, part-time teacher at an adult education centre. Married to Richard.

Richard   Thirty-six. Consultant obstetrician and this year's honorary chairman of the Dead Funny Society.

Brian   Fifty-nine. Cheerful, slightly camp, founder and vice-chairman of the Dead Funny Society.

Nick   Thirty-six. Secondary school teacher of sciences. Member of the society. Married to Lisa.

Lisa   Thirty-three. Ex-dancer. Housewife, mother and member of the society.

Setting

Eleanor and Richard's living room in north London, or any up-market area bordering on city suburbs. Nice furnishings, a view to the front door. Door to kitchen. Door to rest of house. Television with video. Hanging human skeleton. Medical model of human torso with detachable organs. Framed mementoes of dead comedians.

Those to whom this should be dedicated would probably prefer to remain anonymous. But they have my undying affection.

Dead Funny was premièred at the Hampstead Theatre, London on 27 January 1994 with the following cast:

Eleanor	Zoë Wanamaker
Richard	David Haig
Brian	Niall Buggy
Lisa	Beatie Edney
Nick	Danny Webb

Directed by	Terry Johnson
Designed by	Sue Plummer
Lighting design by	Simon Opie
Sound design by	John A Leonard

Artistic Director, Hampstead Theatre	Jenny Topper

Act One

Scene One

Eleanor *sits, motionless. On the floor, scattered toys and the torso, its organs spilled.* **Richard** *enters.*

Richard One night only. Wimbledon Theatre. Sunday night. Norman Wisdom. Norman Wisdom.

Eleanor Lucky Wimbledon.

Richard One night only.

Eleanor Might have been a whole week.

Richard Mr Grimsdale!

Eleanor You got a ticket?

Richard I got twelve.

Eleanor Handy. When you fall asleep you can stretch out.

Richard Don't laugh at me, 'cos I'm a fool.

Eleanor *laughs, softly and ironically.*

Richard What are you doing?

Eleanor Not hoovering up that digestive biscuit.

Richard *finds the torso.*

Richard Bloody hell, Eleanor.

Eleanor What?

Richard This isn't a toy.

Eleanor It's fun to play with.

Richard I don't like it being touched.

Eleanor If you don't want it touched put it somewhere it can't be touched.

Richard I've had this since my father died.

Richard *finds scattered organs, sits to replace them in torso.*

Eleanor I know; I live with it. And that.

Richard Don't start.

Eleanor Well, isn't it about time he was given a decent burial? Couldn't you help him through the pearly loft hatch and up to attic heaven?

Richard It's an antique.

Eleanor No Richard, a chair is an antique. A porcelein doll is an antique. Some poor Victorian sod's fibula is not an antique. God, it gives me the creeps.

Richard What it gives you is an uncomfortable sense of your own mortality.

Eleanor I'll give you an uncomfortable sense of your own mortality one of these days. I'll give you a permanent bloody sense of your own mortality!

Richard The heart's missing.

Another ironic laugh from **Eleanor**

Richard Jesus.

Eleanor Do you realise how old I am?

Pause.

Eleanor I'm three years older than you.

Richard You know I can never . . .

Eleanor You must.

Richard Remember.

Eleanor Everyone knows how old they are.

Richard I'm . . . 37.

Eleanor 38.

Richard 38.

Eleanor Time just passes you by, doesn't it? While the rest of us get dragged along. It's half-past nine.

Richard So what?

Eleanor It is late, Richard.

Richard Don't call me Richard.

Eleanor That's your name.

Richard I know, but I don't like you calling me it. Look, I went to a pub. I had a drink.

Eleanor Why tonight?

Richard Why not?

Eleanor In case you've forgotten which I don't think you have, it's Wednesday.

She stands, hands him the heart of the torso, then gathers toys.

Richard I know.

Eleanor Well then.

Richard Well then what?

Eleanor You know what!

Richard This is broken. Look, he's bloody well broken it.

Eleanor Then you shouldn't leave it lying around to get broken.

Richard I didn't leave it lying around; I left it in a perfectly appropriate place.

Eleanor I hate that word. Appropriate. You never stop using it.

Richard Because it's often the most appropriate word, presumably.

Eleanor And that one; presumably.

Richard If my vocabulary annoys you so much, why do you insist on having these cryptic fucking conversations?

Eleanor Presumably, Richard, because I think it's appropriate to do so. Richard.

Richard Don't try to be cleverer than you are.

Eleanor This is deliberate, isn't it? You're picking a fight.

Richard I've had a difficult day.

Eleanor Putting stuff between us. Pushing me away.

Richard I've just done five hysterectomies. I really don't need this.

Eleanor What?

Richard All this.

Eleanor How were they?

Richard What?

Eleanor The hysterectomies.

Richard What do you mean, how were they?

Eleanor How were they?

Richard Uncomplicated.

Eleanor And the patients?

Richard Unconscious.

Eleanor Can you remember their names?

Richard Whose names?

Eleanor When you're up to your wrists in someone . . .

Richard Eleanor . . .

Eleanor Is she still . . . Jennifer Simpson or is it just offal and chops?

Richard What's wrong with you?

Eleanor What were their names? These unconscious women whose uncomplicated wombs you whipped out today. I want their names.

Pause.

Eleanor You don't know, do you?

Richard Of course I know.

Eleanor Go on then; tell me their names.

Richard Christ, you're in a mood.

Eleanor I knew you didn't know them.

Richard I know them.

Eleanor You don't.

Richard *puts the broken heart in place and closes the torso.* **Eleanor** *winds and sets an alarm clock.*

Richard A drink would be nice.

Eleanor I know you. You'll let it get later and later.

Richard I haven't eaten.

Eleanor That's all right, I haven't cooked. Any more excuses?

Richard I've got a varooca.

Eleanor Did you bring a note from home?

Richard Eleanor.

Eleanor What?

Richard I'm not in the mood.

Eleanor Well, you never will be. Will you? That's the point, isn't it?

Richard It just doesn't feel right . . .

Eleanor I know it doesn't feel right. If it felt right we wouldn't have to do this. It's only an hour of your precious life.

Richard Every other evening.

Eleanor Twice a week.

Richard For how long?

Eleanor That's up to you, isn't it?

Richard If it was up to me we wouldn't be doing it. If it was up to me we'd be watching television.

Eleanor You're doing this deliberately.

Richard Doing what?

Eleanor Making me angry. Making it impossible.

Richard Eleanor . . .

Eleanor Why am I Eleanor all of a sudden? I've been Ellie for ten years and all of a sudden I'm Eleanor. I'm only Eleanor when you're being deliberately provocative.

Richard Don't lose your temper.

Eleanor And if you tell me not to then you think I will, don't you? Don't you!

Richard I won't say another word.

Eleanor Oh, that'll get her, won't it? A bit of martyred silence. That'll make her so bloody angry she'll forget her own name let alone what day it is! Won't she? That'd suit you, wouldn't it?

Richard Yes, that's right, whatever you say.

Eleanor Then agree with her. Stay very calm and agree with her and she'll hit the fucking ceiling! I WILL NOT GET ANGRY WITH YOU, YOU MANIPULATIVE SOD!!!

Richard Do you want to come on Sunday?

Eleanor What?

Richard Norman Wisdom?

She takes a deep breath.

Richard Should I keep a ticket for you?

Eleanor *laughs dangerously. She gets a bottle of gin, a bottle of martini, and a glass. Pours a glug of each and drinks.*

Richard I'm tired, that's all.

Eleanor Hard fucking luck.

Richard Please. Stop swearing.

Eleanor (*quietly*) Pig-faced cunt.

Richard I beg your pardon?

Eleanor I called my headmistress that once, back in the days when I occasionally expressed myself.

Richard Can I have one of those?

She pours another.

Eleanor You think you're tired. I'm exhausted. It's been want want want all day.

Richard Mmm?

Eleanor The baby.

Richard Oh.

Eleanor Apparently this is the first time they've been out together since he was born. Lisa looks as if she hasn't slept for a month. I've only ever sat on sleeping babies before today; I'd no idea. He screamed from five oclock 'till half past seven. Didn't want milk, didn't want cuddles, certainly didn't want me. . . .

Richard I don't envy them.

Eleanor Incessant noise from one end and packets of poo from the other.

Richard Vile.

Eleanor Gorgeous.

Drinks the martini herself.

Eleanor I'm thirty-nine.

Richard I know.

She massages his shoulders.

Richard What's this? Affection or instruction?

Eleanor What does it feel like?

Richard Like you doing what you've been told.

Hits him.

Richard Ow.

Eleanor I thought of that all by myself.

Richard No physical contact without previous consent.

Eleanor You asked for it.

Richard I'll tell the headmistress.

Eleanor I wish you'd take this seriously.

Richard I can't take Miriam seriously.

Eleanor Not her, us.

She drinks, sits next to him.

Eleanor State the parameters.

Richard What?

Eleanor You know the procedure.

Richard We both know the parameters.

Eleanor Miriam said we should state them.

Richard All right then, state them.

Eleanor You state them.

Richard I can't remember them.

Eleanor One hour alone together. Say it.

Richard One hour alone together.

Eleanor This week we touch. But we may not have intercourse.

Richard Fuck, she said.

Eleanor We may not fuck.

Richard Do you think she ever has?

Eleanor Who?

Richard Miriam. I can't imagine it. Make love to Miriam, you might never be seen again.

Eleanor Please concentrate.

Richard We may not fuck. We may touch.

Eleanor How may we touch?

Richard We may touch each other anywhere but the genitals.

Eleanor No.

Richard No?

Eleanor That was last week.

Richard And this week's something else, is it?

Eleanor This week we may touch each other anywhere, but neither must feel it necessary to climax in the other's company.

Richard I think I'm taking this very seriously, wouldn't you say so?

Eleanor Would you like to undress me?

Richard No, thank you.

Eleanor Would you like me to undress you? Richard?

Richard At one of my birthday parties; seventh, eight; my mother made us play a game called Marks and Spencers. We're stood in two long rows and my mother calls out shoe or sock or vest and the first team to get whatever it is into this cardboard box gets a point. I throw one of my sandals in, but I can't say I enjoy it much. There's all these mothers cheering us on and suddenly mine, in a frenzy of encouragement, rips my T-shirt off. I'm left standing there, all thin arms and goosepimples.

Eleanor But that was so long ago. Maybe you should . . .

Richard What?

Eleanor Maybe you should go to an analyst.

Richard No, no no no. My mother should have gone to an analyst. Another time she and my father stole my trousers. We're playing around, Sunday afternoon, suddenly I'm standing in the middle of the carpet in my white cotton underpants. I desperately want my trousers and they won't give them to me.

Eleanor You should tell someone all this.

Richard There's nothing wrong with me.

Eleanor Richard . . .

Richard Don't call me Richard.

Eleanor Sorry. Sweetheart. Darling. Love. You don't have to do anything you don't want to. Now get undressed.

He undresses. She reciprocates.

Richard I've lost a button on this.

Eleanor It's in the pot next to the wok.

He hesitates.

Eleanor Would it help if I went upstairs and slipped into something extremely uncomfortable?

Richard No thanks. You're fine as you are.

He sits in his underpants. She flicks his underpants elastic. He removes them.

Eleanor How do you feel?

Richard Naked.

Eleanor Why?

Richard ?

Eleanor I'm your wife.

Richard I'm stark naked.

Eleanor Or I'm supposed to be.

Richard So what am I supposed to feel?

Eleanor Just . . .

Richard Ecstatic?

Eleanor Try to relax.

Richard I feel fat, that's what I feel.

Eleanor You're not fat.

Richard What's that then?

Eleanor It's nice. I like it.

Richard That apple falling on Newton's head is a myth, you know. I'll tell you how he discovered gravity; on his thirty-fourth birthday he got out of the bath and there it was.

Eleanor I think you've got a lovely body.

Richard You think I should do hen nights?

Eleanor Well it's not so much a Chippendale; more a comfy sofa.

Richard Can I put it away please?

Eleanor Stop talking. Lie down. Relax.

She massages him.

Richard This is your idea of an erotic encounter, is it?

Eleanor Yes; if I was twenty-seven, on a beach in Jamaica. With someone else. Joke.

Richard Ho ho.

Eleanor Mirian said the crucial thing is to relax.

Richard I'd lay good money Miriam's never even done it.

Eleanor Close your eyes.

Richard That's probably why she's a therapist. Figures sooner or later she'll get a patient who's desperate enough to proposition her.

Eleanor Turn over.

Richard Do I have to?

Eleanor Please.

He turns over.

Eleanor What would you like?

Richard I'd like to get dressed.

Eleanor No. Imagine you're on a beach somewhere.

Richard I hate the beach.

Eleanor Why?

Richard Because they make you take your clothes off. Oh, just touch it, will you?

Eleanor What?

Richard You're going everywhere but. Just touch it.

Eleanor Do you mind?

Richard Phone Nick and Lisa. Get a few people round; let everyone take turns.

Eleanor I'm supposed to be allowed to touch it.

Richard Then will you touch it, for Christ's sake.

Eleanor Oh, this is ridiculous.

Richard I know it's ridiculous. I feel ridiculous.

He starts dressing.

Eleanor No.

He stops.

Richard Ellie, please.

Eleanor Not yet. Lie down.

He lies down.

Eleanor Close your eyes.

He closes his eyes. She touches his penis. The doorbell rings.

Eleanor I don't believe it.

Richard That was amazing.

Eleanor I do not believe it.

Richard How did you make it do that?

Eleanor We don't have visitors. When was the last time we had a visitor?

Bell rings again.

Richard That is incredible; you were nowhere near it that time.

He starts getting dressed.

Eleanor Who is it?

Richard How should I know?

Eleanor You've invited someone over, haven't you?

Richard No.

Eleanor You scheming sod. It'll be one of the society with a newsletter proof under his arm. 'Hello Ellie, sorry to disturb you; is Richard in?'

Richard Ellie . . .

Eleanor It'll be Brian. That's who it'll be.

Richard Hold on a minute . . !

He struggles to get dressed. She opens the door.

Brian Hello Ellie, sorry to disturb you; is Richard in?

Eleanor Hello Brian. Come on through.

Richard Hold on.

Enter **Brian**.

Brian I thought about phoning but then I thought not. Oh. Hello Richard.

Richard Hi, Brian.

Brian Sorry, have I disturbed you?

Richard No. No. I was just . . . um.

Eleanor Getting dressed.

Brian Right you are. As one does.

Eleanor He gets home from work Brian and he can't keep his hands off me.

Brian Oh, I see. Sorry Richard.

Richard It's all right.

Brian Shall I come back later?

Eleanor No! Don't leave me alone with him Brian; he's an animal. Besides, it's very stimulating.

Brian What is?

Eleanor Being interrupted.

Brian Oh.

Eleanor Your popping in and out has given us a lot of pleasure over the years.

Brian Oh well, anything to oblige.

Richard What do you want, Brian?

Brian You haven't heard then?

Richard Heard what?

Brian I thought I'd be the first. I have the radio on, you see.

Richard Heard what?

Brian This is going to come as a bit of a shock.

Richard What?

Brian Rather than tell you over the phone.

Richard What?

Brian There's no easy way to say this.

Richard Just say it.

Brian Benny's dead.

Richard What?

Brian He's dead. They found him this afternoon.

Richard Jesus.

Sits.

Richard Benny.

Brian Benny.

Eleanor Benny?

Brian Yep.

Eleanor Benny who?

Brian Benny who!

Richard Benny who?!

Brian Benny Hill.

Eleanor Oh, thank God for that. I thought it was someone we knew.

Brian Being Chairman I thought you'd better know A.S.A.P.

Richard Thanks Bri. I don't believe it.

Brian Nor do I.

Richard Benny Hill.

Brian It's hard to believe. He was found at home.

Richard Heart?

Brian Yep.

Richard Hmm.

Brian That's what I was thinking, Eric, Tommy, Sid. What is it about a comedian's heart?

Richard It's the stress, Brian. A stressed heart just wears out sooner. God likes a good laugh.

Brian So he summons the best, I know.

Eleanor Well, thanks for popping over, Brian.

Brian I couldn't have phoned.

Eleanor Got anyone else to tell?

Brian Well, the entire membership should be contacted, really.

Eleanor Well, don't feel you have to stay to comfort us in our grief. You spread the news, we'll comfort each other.

Brian I thought it would be best from the Chairman, really.

Richard You're right. I'll phone round.

Brian I was in the chair when Sid went. I had the honour. Members wept.

Eleanor Sid?

Pause.

All James.

Eleanor . . . sorry.

Richard I'll get on with it.

Eleanor Richard.

Richard Would you like a drink?

Brian I suppose a drink would be appropriate, yes.

Richard You know what I'm thinking?

Brian I think I probably do.

Richard Why oh why . . .

Brian I know.

Richard Why would he not appear live?

Brian That's . . .

Richard Eh?

Brian Exactly. Everyone agreed. Benny should have appeared live.

Eleanor He'll have a bit of a job from now on, won't he?

Richard Ellie.

Eleanor What?

Brian You don't understand, Ellie. You see, the man was music hall.

Richard He was.

Brian You can draw a line . . .

Richard A direct line from the greats. From Max Miller . . .

Brian Further.

Richard Further.

Brian From Little Tich . . .

Richard From Dan Leno.

Brian Dan Leno!

Richard You can draw a straight line from Dan Leno through Little Tich, Max Miller, Jimmy James . . . all the way to Benny.

Brian But he wouldn't do live.

Richard He wouldn't.

Eleanor I bet he would now.

Brian And that is a tragedy.

Richard And. It's one more nail . . .

Brian I know.

Richard . . . In the coffin of music hall.

Brian That is . . .

Richard Mm?

Brian Absolutely. True.

Eleanor Well Brian, I can tell that at a time like this you'd probably prefer to be alone . . .

Richard Here you go.

Brian What's this then?

Richard It's a martini.

Brian Oh.

Richard To Benny.

Brian To Benny.

Richard I'm not going to make a speech.

Eleanor *hides her head.*

Richard Just suffice it to say . . . thanks for making us laugh.

Brian Benny.

Richard Benny.

Eleanor I thought you were the DEAD Funny Society.

Richard Yes?

Eleanor Well shouldn't you be celebrating this? Lord knows the rest of the country probably is.

Richard Eleanor! Sorry, Brian.

Eleanor It Was A Joke. Of course, neither of you would recognise a joke that didn't have its trousers round its ankles.

Richard Don't talk comedy to us.

Eleanor I wouldn't try to get a word in edgeways.

Richard You have . . . she has absolutely no sense of humour.

Eleanor If I had no sense of humour I would have hung myself from the bannisters on our third wedding anniversary, which in case you've forgotten, we celebrated with a trip to Little and Large. Believe me, I have a sense of humour. I do.

Brian I'd better be off then.

Richard Right. I'll ring round.

Brian And we'll give him a bit of a send-off one night next week, shall we?

Richard Good idea.

Brian Wednesday?

Richard Well, why not?

Eleanor Wednesday?

Brian No one does much on a Wednesday.

Eleanor Lord knows we don't.

Brian Wednesday then. Anyway, sorry to disturb you. I'll let you get on, nudge nudge say no more. Then again, you're probably not in the mood any more. I'll see myself out.

Eleanor Don't slam the door; there's a baby upstairs.

Brian That was quick.

Richard Nick and Lisa's.

Eleanor Just put it on the latch and pull it to.

Brian Will do. Well sir, this is Fred Scuttle saying I'll be seeing you, sir.

Laugh. Silence.

Brian Sad day.

Eleanor I think that just about says it, Brian.

Richard Bye, Brian.

Brian Bye.

Exit **Brian**.

Eleanor How did his mother know?

Richard What?

Eleanor He was just a tiny baby when she named him; how could she possibly have known?

Richard There was no need to be rude. These guys care.

Eleanor So do you.

Richard Yes, so do I

Eleanor That's what worries me.

Richard What unites us is a very simple thing.

Eleanor Mmm hmm?

Richard Alien to you, of course. Risible as far as you're concerned.

Eleanor Try me.

Richard The joy of simple laughter.

Pause.

Eleanor No, I can't think of anything to say to that.

Richard What are you doing?

Eleanor Putting the clock back.

Richard Ellie.

Eleanor What?

Richard Benny Hill died today.

Eleanor But Richard, life, however impoverished, must go on.

Richard You're obsessed.

Eleanor You're sitting there mourning Benny Hill I'm obsessed? He's probably watching you now. Sitting on a cloud with a television remote in one hand and his penis in the other. Come on Richard, he's saying. Give her one for me.

Richard I've got a lot of phone calls to make.

Eleanor Now?

Richard Yes, now.

He phones. **Eleanor** *puts on a video.*

Richard Hello, Toby? Richard. Bit of bad news, mate. Benny Hill passed away. Yes. I know you were. Yes. Look, there's a bit of a do at my place next Wednesday. Eight o'clock. Yes. Hard for it to sink in straight away, isn't it? Yes.

Miriam (*video*) Hello, my name's Miriam Fairchild. I've been helping loving couples improve their intimate lives for over twenty years, and I hope this video will help you improve yours.

Richard Yes, absolutely. I must um . . . phone round the others. Bye then.

Miriam (*video*) While you watch, we're going to share some of the tenderest moments of sexual expression with three loving couples. Remember our couples are not actors, but genuine loving couples who have volunteered to share with us what they would normally only share between themselves.

Richard What is she doing in my living room? Hello Tracey, is Dave there?

Miriam (*video*) We're going to watch as they explore each other's bodies and as they experiment to bring to each other those gifts of sensual experience that only sex between a loving couple can offer.

Richard What is she doing on my television set?

Eleanor It's the one she mentioned. I got it in Smiths.

She stops the video. He phones. She fast-forwards.

Richard Dave? Bit of bad news, mate. Oh, you've heard. Right. Yes. Yes. Well, a bit of a do at my place next Wednesday. Eight o'clock.

She turns on the video again. Jolly sensual background music.

Richard Yeh. Yeh. Yeh.

Cockney Woman (*video*) When Phil first touched my vagina he didn't really know his way about, but since then I've used my own fingers and his to help him learn about all its different parts and what gives me most pleasure.

Richard Bloody hell. Sorry, not you, I was um . . . I'll see you and your wife next week then, Phil. I mean Dave. And Tracey, yes. Cheers then, bye.

Cockney Man (*video*) What I've found out is most important is to be gentle and understanding, not go at it like a bull in a china shop sort of thing. And to keep a steady rhythm.

Cockney Woman (*video*) What I really love is for Phil to use his tongue. I think at first we were both afraid of oral sex, but now it's quite a favourite. In fact sometimes that's all we do for an entire evening.

Eleanor Jesus.

Richard Bloody hell.

Eleanor Is she really doing that?

Richard Well where's it gone if she isn't?

Miriam (*video*) Above all, it's important for a couple to talk to each other.

Eleanor Unless they've got their mouths full of course.

Miriam (*video*) Don't be afraid to tell your partner exactly what pleases you most.

Cockney Man (*video*) Foreplay's a movable feast really. Sometimes it lasts a long time and sometimes we both get aroused really quickly.

Eleanor They're going to, aren't they?

Richard I've read about this couple.

Cockney Woman (*video*) Making love to Phil has become over time the most exciting thing in my life.

Eleanor My . . . God.

Cockney Woman (*video*) It's brought us closer, and helped us to a greater understanding of one another as human beings.

Richard They met at the audition, apparently.

Eleanor Don't be ridiculous.

Richard It's true.

Eleanor He hasn't got a condom on.

They watch. Enter **Nick**, *quietly, intending to surprise them. Freezes.*

Cockney Woman (*video*) Whenever I find myself approaching orgasm now I feel free to really let myself go. And so does Phil.

Sound of approaching climaxes. **Nick** *very quietly tries to creep backwards out of the room.* **Lisa** *enters behind him.*

Lisa Only us.

Richard *and* **Eleanor** *leap up, fumble for the remote, and turn off the TV.*

Richard Hi.

Nick Hi.

Eleanor Hello, Nick.

Lisa Hi. Is he all right?

Eleanor Who?

Lisa The baby.

Richard Baby?

Eleanor What baby?

Lisa My baby.

Eleanor Oh, he's fine. Fast asleep.

Nick Sorry if we er . . .

Lisa I said you'd scare the daylights out of them. It's about time he grew up. Lord knows what you might have been doing, privacy of your own home.

Nick The door was on the latch.

Eleanor We were just . . . watching TV.

Nick Were you?

Richard Yes, just um . . .

Eleanor A programme.

Richard A video.

Eleanor A video.

Richard A programme.

Nick I'd only just come in, I was um . . .

Richard Some rubbish, anyway.

Nick Right. Wednesdays.

Lisa What were you watching?

Nick I love this rug. Lisa? Haven't you always loved this rug?

Lisa Umm.

Nick Great rug.

Lisa It's a lovely rug, yes.

Nick And so much nicer on the wall than it would be on the floor.

Richard Well, we like it there, anyway.

Eleanor At least you can't trip over it.

Lisa I like a nice video. What did you get out?

Richard There's always a flaw, of course. There's always a deliberate flaw woven into the design so as not to offend the perfection of Allah.

Nick Really?

Lisa Comedy or horror?

Eleanor Of course in this one there's a number of flaws.

Nick What does that signify?

Eleanor A cheap carpet.

They laugh. **Lisa** *moves away from the rug.*

Lisa Nice evening indoors, a glass of wine and a good video.

Nick There's a flaw. Look.

Lisa Lovely.

Nick Look.

Lisa I've looked.

Nick No, but look.

Lisa They've got a lot of lovely things, Nick. I've always said, the way Ellie's decorated this house makes me wish we had the same taste.

She picks up the cassette box, looks at it, turns it upside down, drops it.

Lisa And you're right about the rug; it's beautiful. I especially like this little bit down here. Oh look, there's a little cat.

Eleanor Camel.

Lisa Camel.

Richard Anyway.

Lisa Anyway.

Nick Right.

Richard Drinks!

Nick Lovely.

Lisa Sorry if we're a bit early.

Nick Didn't stay for the second half.

Richard What did you go and see?

Nick *Starlight Express*.

Richard Not very good?

Nick Oh no, excellent. Excellent. Gave Lisa a headache.

Lisa It wasn't the show, Nick. When I get a headache it's for a reason.

Richard Right.

Lisa I immediately think; something's wrong.

Nick She immediately thought; Ellie's dropped the baby down the stairs.

Lisa No I didn't.

Nick That's what you said.

Lisa No I didn't.

Nick Ellie's fed the baby bleach instead of apple juice and buried it in the garden.

Lisa Nick. Ellie, I trust you completely, or I wouldn't have left him in the first place. You're really getting on my nerves lately. Where is he?

Eleanor Under the lawn just beside the cherry tree. It's a lovely spot.

Lisa When you become a mother Ellie, you'll realise; certain things aren't funny any more.

Nick Husbands. Life.

Eleanor He's fine. He's upstairs. Do you need a paracetamol?

Lisa Oh no, I just have to wait 'til it passes.

Richard You won't have heard the news then.

Nick What?

Richard Benny Hill.

Nick What?

Richard Died.

Nick No.

Richard Yep.

Nick What a bloody shame.

Lisa I knew it.

Richard What?

Lisa My headache.

Nick Don't be ridiculous.

Lisa Whenever I get a headache like that, somebody somewhere dies.

Nick Statistically speaking of course, a few million more peg it every time you blow your nose.

Eleanor What's wrong with you?

Lisa One of the chorus skated over his cellphone.

Richard Cellphone?

Nick Month's trial.

Lisa I think I'll go and see our son.

Eleanor I'll show you.

Lisa No one ever phones you at home, let alone somewhere else. He's had it a fortnight; it hasn't rung yet.

Exit **Lisa** *and* **Eleanor**.

Nick Poor old Benny. He'll have left a few bob.

Richard I should think so.

Nick Mean old bugger apparently. Worse than Doddy.

Richard Fear. That's what it is.

Nick Fear?

Richard That the crowd'll turn, the laughter stop. Fear of penury.

Nick Look at Frankie.

Richard Perfect example.

Nick Out of work 1957 to 1963, then again all through the eighties. And that's a man with staggering talent.

Richard Must be frightening.

Nick I should say so. Yes missus. I've never been so insulted. Oh . . .

Both Please yourselves.

Nick Bit sexist of course, Benny Hill.

Richard Not in an offensive way, though.

Nick No, no. I meant in a women-with-big-tits-and-short-skirts-bending-over-a-lot sort of way.

Richard Absolutely.

Nick Nice work if you can get it. I'll bet he died with a smile on his face.

Richard How is work?

Nick I can't stand it. And I'm earning a pittance. I should have studied harder you know, when we were young. You shouldn't have encouraged me to be such a nerd. I mean if you got through med. school, anyone could have.

Richard You put on some good revues.

Nick I should have studied. I've got the brain you know.

Richard It wasn't your brain got you thrown out; it was the May ball.

Nick It was class prejudice.

Richard It was the penis sewn to the inside of your trouser leg.

Nick I was going to put it back. It's not as if one borrowed dick was going to halt the advance of medical science. I could have been a surgeon.

Richard Oh, you showed great promise.

Nick I mean admit it; it's not that difficult. Takes more bottle than skill. A car mechanic knows more than a surgeon; he knows his way around a Ford, a Vauxhall, a Toyota. But bodies; been inside one, been inside them all. Find the bit that's not working and whip it out. I could do that. There's nothing I don't know about a Vauxhall Astra.

Richard You're better off out of it.

Nick Or the Cavalier.

Richard It gets you down in the end.

Nick Falling apart, of course.

Richard What?

Nick The Astra.

Richard Oh.

Nick And I'm thirty-seven!

Richard Don't you start.

Nick They've put me in charge of the sixth-form. Two boys, eleven girls. I'm not joking Richard, these girls. I mean it's nine-thirty on a Tuesday morning and I've got to get from registration to the science block with a hard on the size of a chalk duster.

Richard Tricky.

Nick Especially when you're teaching a class of seventeen-year-olds what one is. And this National Curriculum's a bit bloody specific. I used to whap on the old Shell video and leave the rest to filter down from the back row. Now we have to discuss it within a moral frame of reference. I'd rather discuss it in the back of the Astra. With Bradshaw, Emma.

Richard You wouldn't, would you?

Nick I did once.

Richard Really?

Nick Never again. Trouble with seventeen-year-olds; they're so bloody immature. And prudish when you get down to it.

Richard Bit of a risk, wasn't it?

Nick Came a bit close. Luckily she needed two B's and a C to do Chemistry at Hull. Promised not to wreck my career if I fiddled her multiple choice. Never again. It's not just the money I envy you; it's all those nurses I regret. Nurses know what's what.

Richard I wouldn't know.

Nick Can I borrow this?

Cellphone rings. **Nick** *answers it eagerly.*

Nick Excuse me. Hello? Hello? Ah.

Richard What?

Nick Battery. Tells you when it needs re-charging.

Richard Really?

Nick Oh yes. It's very user-friendly.

Richard *takes the phone.* **Eleanor** *and* **Lisa** *return, the latter with carry cot.*

Lisa Here he is then. Fast asleep.

Nick Fully networked; take it anywhere.

Richard Uhuh.

Lisa Thanks, Ellie.

Eleanor That's all right. Any time.

Nick Twelve number memory, call back; the lot.

Richard Nice and light.

Nick Oh, yes.

Lisa Oh, look.

Eleanor He's lovely.

Lisa He is, isn't he? Nick, look.

Nick Yeh.

Lisa Look, Richard.

Richard Right.

Lisa Have a look. Sweet. He's so sweet. You've got your mummy's mouth, haven't you?

Nick Certainly has.

Lisa But you've got your Daddy's eyes. He's got your eyes, Nick.

Nick He's got your father's nose. (*Laughs*) Hya hya hya.

Richard What?

Lisa Nick.

Nick Thirty-two quid a month, plus airtime.

Lisa It's hard sometimes, for fathers to bond. They haven't been through the pain, you see. They haven't got the chemicals. When you give birth Ellie, when you give life . . . it's . . . well, you feel connected to something that, well, goes on beyond your own . . . I don't know . . . your past, or your future. You become more . . . what's the word? Mortal, or the other thing; I can never remember the word. Anyway; you know you'll never be the same again. It's so . . . it's really, it's. . . .

Nick Can I use those jump leads?

Richard Sure. They're in my boot.

Lisa We'd better get him home.

Richard I'll give you a hand.

Nick Thanks, mate.

Lisa I'll bring him out when it's going.

The men leave.

Lisa I didn't say what he said I said. About you dropping the baby, not downstairs.

Eleanor I'm sure you didn't.

Lisa It's strange though, when you're a little bit psychic. You know when something happens, but not always exactly what. Until later.

Eleanor I see.

Lisa (*mouths*) How are things?

Eleanor What?

Lisa (*mouths*) How are things?

Eleanor Things are fine, except I seem to have just gone deaf. What things?

Lisa Things, you know.

Eleanor Worse if anything.

Lisa Nick's got very strange since the baby.

Eleanor Oh, we'll sort something out.

Lisa You need a common interest, that's what you need. That's what Nick and I have. Not just the society; we've cultivated many common interests. We've got dozens of common interests.

Well at least I have. Nick's a bit moody at the moment; he's not got much interest in anything. Why don't you come to an appreciation evening? It really is great fun. When we put up Hattie's plaque in Ickenham it was really moving. And Mrs Gardner, she's not a member but she's the lady who lives in the house where Hattie was born and she was very supportive, she invited us all in and she'd been to the video shop and got out *Carry on Matron* and we all sat and watched and Ellie, we laughed. And Richard was wearing the matron's cap; you know, the one that Hattie wore that my mum had in her cabinet; oh, he looked a sight, but anyway he turned to me and he said, 'You know Lisa, I wish Ellie was here.'

Eleanor Did he?

Lisa Mmmm.

Eleanor No he didn't. God, you're a terrible liar.

Lisa Well, he had a look on his face as much as to say.

Eleanor I've tried joining in; you know that. It's hopeless. I don't find anything funny any more.

Lisa Well Ellie, humour's a funny thing. In my experience men will laugh at anything, whereas women wait to see if the men laugh and then sort of jump in. Except at certain jokes, usually about S.E.X. when the women all laugh and the men just look at them. I speak of course as the only female member of the society.

Eleanor I don't know how you can bear them all en masse.

Lisa Oh I know; all those men. I wonder what I think I'm doing there sometimes. I suppose it's just . . . well, you know; when you've been in the business.

Eleanor You only danced for three summer seasons.

Lisa I did sketches too.

Eleanor In Bournemouth.

Lisa Library sketch. Hospital sketch. Big breaths, nurse. And I'm only theventeen. And my mum was in showbusiness all her life.

Eleanor It's in your blood, I know.

Lisa All those Carry Ons. I pointed her out in *Carry On Matron*; she's in the bed by the door whenever they walk past. The men loved that you see. That's why I like to turn up. I'm a sort of link for them; to the real thing.

Eleanor You're the least they deserve.

Richard *enters*.

Richard Well, it's going. I'd get in quick if I were you.

Lisa Ooh, right. Listen Ellie, thanks again.

Eleanor Any time.

Lisa And thank you Richard.

Richard That's all right.

Lisa Bye then.

Richard Bye.

Eleanor *shows her out.*

Lisa And remember what I said.

Eleanor I will. Bye.

Lisa Bye.

Eleanor *returns*.

Richard What did she say?

Eleanor If what Lisa said went in one ear and out the other it would be a blessing. Unfortunately it goes in one ear, and bounces round the cranium for hours.

Richard What were you talking about?

Eleanor Not you.

Richard Good. I think I'll turn in.

Eleanor Well, it is way past your bedtime. I bought this Mills and Boon today for fifty pee. Look. That's you and me on the front, the day we met. You were handsome, you had a crooked smile, and you were wearing a white coat with a stethoscope sticking out of the pocket.

He takes the book.

Eleanor Well, it's almost us. She hasn't got her feet in stirrups, of course. When I was untangling my knickers from my tights and you asked me out to dinner, was it love at first sight?

Richard No, it was serious professional misconduct.

Eleanor Because you had a stethoscope I presumed you were a humanitarian. Because you smiled I presumed you had a sense of humour. But you haven't; you've a clinical obsession with it. Because you were handsome I presumed you were sexy, but you've turned out about as sexy as Ernie Wise. Which of course you'll probably take as a compliment.

Richard I wish you'd listen to yourself sometimes.

Eleanor I do. I know. I sound like that poor old cow in all those second-rate sitcoms. The one who's desperate to sleep with Reg Varney. Or Sid or Benny or some other fat ugly bastard. Only one joke and it's always on her, because they're not interested. They don't want her. They want the pneumatic bimbo who lives next door.

Richard There's no one else.

Eleanor It's just me then?

Richard It's not you. It's me. It's what I do, it's who I am, it's . . . I don't know.

Eleanor It's not necessarily all your fault.

Richard It is my fault. But it's not my problem. I can only feel what I feel.

Eleanor Nothing for me or nothing at all?

Richard Nothing much.

Eleanor You pursued me with such ardour, such passion. I fought it so hard, loving you. But I did, and I do. And it's indescribably painful trying not to.

He goes to bed. She gets another drink, closes the door and turns on the video. Love-making and music. She watches.

Lights fade.

Segue Scenes One and Two

(*Video voice over*)

Woman I know now which bits he likes touched and what he likes me to do with what and where. Lovemaking is an all-over thing; little strokes, little kisses. Little bites even, if you're very very careful. And sometimes even teasing. You can tease one another for ages and ages, and then stop and not do anything and it's very exciting and a bit frustrating or very frustrating, but it's still enjoyable and still very sexy. And sometimes the next time you make love is, well . . . very special.

Man It really is really really important to get to understand what arouses your partner most. And to do that you've got to talk frankly about each other's bodies. We used to be quite shy, but my partner taught me about what she likes most just by opening up the subject.

Miriam In our younger years, between adolescence and our mid-twenties, we can tend to treat sex as an end in itself rather than a single part of a loving relationship. As a result some of us were first introduced to sex with a series of casual lovers or one night stands. But we must never forget that we all are searching for the same thing; a way of combining the physical pleasures of our shared bodies with a genuine love for another human being. The only truly satisfying sexual life is one that pays dividends in trust, affection, and intimacy.

Scene Two

The same. One week later. **Richard** *alone.*

Richard The comic traditions of this small island are the envy of the world. France has its rural whimsy. America its Jewish wit. Belgium its Belgians. No, but seriously. One nation stands out when it comes to being funny. Ask a Norwegian, a Canadian, a native Australian, they'll all tell you; the English are funny. And the undisputed King of British comedy was of course, indeed still is . . . Benny Hill.

Eleanor *appears listening.*

Richard But it's not only those Joe Soaps, those Mr and Mrs Averages who number themselves among his fans. Mention should also be made of Greta Garbo. Michael Jackson. The Queen Mother.

Eleanor The Ayatollah Khomeni. Saddam Hussein.

Richard I didn't know you were in.

Eleanor I fell asleep.

Richard Have you been drinking?

Eleanor I only drink at mealtimes.

Richard What did you have for lunch?

Eleanor Three martinis and an orgasm.

Richard Are you going out?

Eleanor Tonight's the night is it? Farewell Fred Scuttle?

Richard Yes.

Eleanor I wouldn't miss it for the world. I've got a class at seven, but I'll be back!

Richard You're drinking too much.

Eleanor I'm drinking just enough. For a Wednesday.

Richard Don't start.

Eleanor When are the anoraks arriving?

Richard They don't all wear anoraks.

Eleanor They do.

Richard That is a generalisation.

Eleanor Every one of them wears an anorak.

Richard Inaccurate stereotyping.

Eleanor I know they don't call them anoraks anymore, but if it's day-glo and padded and makes you look like a cuddly hand grenade then as far as I'm concerned it's an anorak.

Richard I'm willing to admit not all of them have an IQ of a hundred and fifty . . .

Eleanor Put together.

Richard . . . and it's very easy to take the mickey out of a group of people bonded by a common interest . . .

Eleanor Not in this case. You lot are beyond satire.

Richard . . . but there's no need for this unending stream of abuse.

Eleanor Ooh, you're sexy when you're petulant. I've got a surprise for you later.

Doorbell.

Eleanor Hello, Brian.

Richard *goes to the door.* **Eleanor** *drinks.*

Richard Hello, Brian.

Brian *enters with shopping.*

Brian I'm very upset. I've just had a dreadful row and you know me; I don't have arguments, but he's really upset me.

Richard Who?

Brian Who do you think? Les Rollins.

Richard Ah.

Brian Anyway, I've been to Tescos and I've baked a cake. Hello Ellie.

Eleanor Hello Brian.

Brian What's this?

Eleanor A key to the door; you'll be in and out all evening.

Brian Ooh, only if my luck changes. Ta. Anyway, Rollins phoned me about tonight and says; what's all this he hears about fancy dress? I said it's not fancy dress, it's a token gesture. Token gesture my arse, he says. I'm not coming dressed up! I tried to explain it's a little tradition the society likes to uphold and that it wasn't fancy dress, it was just a visual tribute and you didn't have to go the whole hog. Just a beret or some rimless specs or slicked back hair and chinese glasses, whatever . . . a *tribute*.

Richard That's right.

Brian Well, he wouldn't have it. Said it was farcical. I was a bit rude; I said; if you don't like it, don't come.

Eleanor Maybe he's got a point.

Brian What?

Eleanor Well. It's a bit undignified, isn't it?

Brian There is nothing undignified about humbling oneself and donning the symbolic garb of a great clown.

Richard Of course not.

Eleanor It's just that some people look a bit funny dressed up in a false nose, silly specs and baggy trousers; not you Brian, but some people.

Brian You think he's right?! You think we should abandon one of our silliest traditions just because Les Rollins 'feels a bit peculiar'?! He likes Ben Elton, you know. Les Rollins is a big fan of Ben Elton. What does that tell you?

Richard Don't get upset, Brian.

Brian I am upset. I'm very upset. Ever since he joined there's been contention in the air. I knew he was going to be trouble when he turned up to his first meeting with that video of Tommy Cooper's last performance. I was appalled.

Richard There was quite a healthy majority wanted to see it, Brian.

Eleanor Seventeen to one, wasn't it?

Brian I was ashamed of you. I thought you at least had good taste. That upset me, that show of hands. I couldn't watch.

Richard You should have. It was actually very dignified.

Eleanor A man holding a rubber chicken having a coronary in front of fifteen hundred people? Dignified?

Brian Exactly.

Richard He was plying his craft, he paused, and then he fell like an oak. Yes. Dignified.

Eleanor It was a hell of a trick, I'll give him that.

Brian It wasn't even a first generation tape; it was a grainy old bootleg.

Richard Bit of history though, Brian.

Brian It was a snuff movie. I knew we'd rue the day we voted Les Rollins in. I'm not at all sure any more about a lot of the membership, to tell you the truth. I've seen the *Bottom* videos surreptitiously passed during coffee break. There doesn't seem to be any discrimination any more between good old bawdy innuendo and filth. Between good old slapstick and sick physical violence. Maybe I'm getting old. He hasn't said anything to you, has he? Rollins?

Richard What about?

Brian Me?

Richard No.

Brian Anyway, that's the bad news.

Eleanor There's good news, is there?

Brian There's very good news. We've got a guest of honour. Don't ask me how I got his phone number, but I did. And you know my philosophy; if you don't ask you don't get. So I phoned and I asked and he said he'd be honoured.

Richard Who?

Brian Honoured. I nearly fell off my chair.

Richard Who?

Brian Henry McGee.

Richard No.

Brian Yes.

Richard Henry McGee?

Brian Yes.

Richard I don't believe you.

Brian Henry McGee.

Eleanor In my house?

Brian He was totally charming. He said of course he'd heard of us. He'd seen us on the news doing Hattie's plaque. And he said he'd be honoured to join with us in remembering Benny.

Richard That's extraordinary.

Brian Then he went a bit quiet. You know.

Richard Right.

Brian Then he said . . . I miss him, of course.

Richard Did he?

Brian I miss him, of course. Then he asked if I'd like to see *It Runs in the Family*. He's currently appearing in *It Runs in the Family*.

Eleanor Benny Hill?

Brian Henry McGee.

Eleanor Oh. I was going to say. In fact, I was going to go.

Brian He said I should definitely see it, Ray Cooney being a master of the genre. And let him know I was coming.

Richard He offered you tickets?

Brian No, just to let him know when I'd got tickets, I suppose to see him afterwards.

Richard That's. . . .

Brian He was very charming on the phone.

Richard I'm not surprised though.

Brian A charming man. 'I miss him, of course.'

Eleanor Well, that's a bit of a coup isn't it, Brian?

Brian I know.

Eleanor Step up from Bella Emberg.

Brian Oh, now now. Bella was . . .

Richard Ellie.

Eleanor Oh, she was.

Brian She was very kind to fit us in to what was for her a pretty hectic Madhouse season.

Eleanor I know. I know. She was very kind. And startlingly articulate. I think Bella Emberg was almost as articulate as she was thin.

Brian Can I unpack this lot in the kitchen?

Richard Of course.

Exit **Brian**.

Eleanor I shouldn't have said that.

Richard You're getting very cruel.

Eleanor I know.

Richard I mean; poor Brian.

Eleanor I mean poor Bella. She was sweet.

Brian (*off*) I've catered for twenty.

Eleanor Twenty?

Brian But if they all turn up there should be enough.

Eleanor You said half a dozen.

Brian (*off*) Oh, and I had a bit of a stroke in Tescos.

Eleanor I bet that had them rolling in the aisles. Where can I get the video?

Brian Look. Custard pies.

Eleanor What for?

Brian Just a joke. I shouldn't think anyone'll actually throw one.

Eleanor I should bloody well hope not.

Brian Do you think it's living dangerously? Because I needn't put them out.

Richard No, it's a nice idea.

Eleanor Very dignified.

Brian Can I help myself to plates?

Richard Yes.

Exit **Brian**.

Richard This means a lot to Brian.

Eleanor So?

Richard Why are you trying to spoil it for him?

Eleanor Time of the month.

Richard Couldn't we call a truce, just for tonight?

Pause.

Eleanor I suppose a fuck's out of the question?

Richard If you're that desperate, have an affair.

Enter **Brian**.

Brian It's very good of you both. I gave serious thought to using my flat now that Mum's not there. But it's so small. I thought if I opened it out and used Mum's room, but that'd feel very strange because I'm not using Mum's room yet. I'm still in the small back room, but I have laid out the dining area in the living room as my office area now. I use the big table and to eat I use the television table I got Mum from Argos. All in all it's nice to have the extra space; I know she wouldn't mind me saying that; she used to say much the same herself. But her room's much as she left it. Which reminds me Ellie, I keep forgetting to bring you that perfume . . .

Eleanor Oh, that's all right.

Brian No no, I've remembered.

Gives her a bottle of stale 4711 and a miniscule bottle of Chanel no. 4.

Brian She'd have liked you to have it. She liked you.

Eleanor Thank you.

Brian I've got some sausage rolls. Can I pop them in the oven?

Eleanor You can pop anything in my oven any time you like, Brian.

Brian Oh well, if you weren't spoken for.

Eleanor I'm not even spoken *to*. Richard wouldn't mind.

Brian Oh well then, I'll whisk you away.

Eleanor Yes please. Thanks for this.

Brian *exits*.

Eleanor Who with?

Richard What?

Eleanor An affair?

Richard Well, that would be your choice, wouldn't it?

Eleanor Oh, thanks. All right. I'll have an affair with Nick.

Richard Nick? You always said he had a face like a turtle.

Eleanor You don't have to look at the mantelpiece, Richard, when you're sitting on it.

Brian *enters*.

Brian Right, that's me done for now. I'm just going to nip home and put my frock on. Nick is bringing the wine now, isn't he?

Richard I hope so.

Brian I'll see you later then. What a performance.

Brian *leaves*.

Richard What I meant was you don't have to lead a celibate life just because I choose to. You are allowed to choose.

Eleanor I chose you. We're supposed to have chosen each other. We're supposed to be a couple. Couples make love.

Richard Not the couples I know.

Eleanor Yes they do.

Richard They don't you know.

Eleanor Well the couples I know do. It's normal.

Richard It doesn't feel normal.

Eleanor It's perfectly normal for most people.

Richard I'm not most people.

Eleanor Exactly; you're not normal.

Richard I'm perfectly normal.

Eleanor If you were normal, we'd have a sex life!

Richard I can't stand these conversations going round and round . . .

Eleanor We have to discuss things; it's part of the process.

Richard Part of the pressure.

Eleanor There is no pressure.

Richard Pressure from Miriam, pressure from you.

Eleanor I don't want to pressure you.

Richard Don't then.

Eleanor But I can't ignore this . . . misery I feel.

Richard This is my body. It's not yours. It's mine. It doesn't want to be touched. That doesn't make me particularly happy, but it feels perfectly normal.

Doorbell.

Eleanor I'm going to rip that doorbell out with my teeth. I gave you the key, Brian!

She goes to the door. **Nick** *and* **Lisa** *enter, with carrycot.*

Eleanor (*off*) Oh. Hello.

Lisa I know we're early, I know. I told him we were going to be early.

Nick Sorry.

Eleanor That's alright; party's started. Come join the fun.

Richard Hi, Nick.

Nick Hi.

Lisa Can I take him straight upstairs?

Eleanor Sure.

Lisa *exits.*

Nick Sorry we're early. Bit of a snag. I couldn't get any cash out of the machine for the booze.

Richard Been embezzling the funds, have you?

Nick No, no. I don't know; it just ate the card. Thing is, we're a bit short ourselves at the moment.

Richard I'll give you some.

Nick Cheers, mate. There's a second card you see, that Brian used to have, but he swears he gave it back to me. Oh, it'll sort itself out. Ta, mate. I'd better rush; I've left the car running.

Eleanor If you're going to Threshers, you can give me a lift to the Poly.

Nick Sure.

Eleanor I'll give you a blow job on the way.

Nick Splendid. She's a wonderful woman, your wife. Nothing's too much trouble, is it?

Richard See you later.

Nick Right. Come on then; be gentle with me.

Exit **Nick**.

Eleanor It'd give him a hell of a shock if I did, wouldn't it?

Richard Go to work, Ellie.

Exit **Ellie**.

Eleanor (*off*) Bye, Lisa!

Lisa (*off*) Oh. Bye.

Richard *puts on a pink satin tie. Enter* **Lisa**.

Lisa She go with him?

Richard She's got a class.

Lisa Oh, I see.

She takes off her coat; dressed in a severe woollen twinset and pearls.

Lisa Da da! Nick wanted me to come as a Hill's Angel of course, but I told him he'd got another think coming. So I've come as a spinster. Well, it was either bimbo, battle axe or spinster and I'm certainly not a battle axe, am I? I've had this headache threatening me all day. Norman Wisdom was very good, wasn't he? I'd have enjoyed it more if I hadn't been stuck on the end next to Les Rollins. He kept saying whatever it was

Norman was going to say just before he said it, and he's a very tactile person, isn't he, Les? Very wide to sit next to. Squeezes past when there's bags of room. Holds his glass at nipple height so he can brush you with his knuckles. He's been paying me quite a lot of attention actually; I've been wondering if I should mention it to Nick.

Richard *moves behind her, caresses her. Lifts her skirt.*

Did you see 'It'll Be Alright on the Night'? Dennis Norden said something very interesting. He said apparently Sigmund Freud said there were only four kinds of joke. I've got it on tape. Apparently . . . let's see if I can get this right . . . there's Concealment of Knowledge Later Revealed, Substitution of One Concept for Another . . .

She bends over the back of the sofa. He undresses her.

Lisa Um . . . oh, Unexpected Conclusion to a Hitherto Logical Progression . . .

He enters her.

Lisa And um . . . something else.

They fuck.

Lisa Hard.

Enter **Benny Hill** *in long mac, beret and pebble glasses.*

Brian Here I am then.

Lisa *head first over the sofa,* **Richard** *zips up fly before first securing penis.*

Brian Only me.

Act Two

Scene One

The same. A moment later.

Brian Mind you; I can't see a thing through these glasses. Oh, hello, Lisa.

Lisa Hello Brian.

Brian How are you?

Lisa I've got a terrible headache.

Brian Poor thing.

Lisa Excuse me.

*Exit **Lisa**, squinting oddly, walking into doorframe.*

Richard She gets these headaches.

Brian Well, some cures are more enjoyable than others, I suppose. Sorry, Richard.

Richard Lisa and I, we're strictly um . . .

Brian Oh, live and let live, me. I may seem old-fashioned, but not a lot surprises me.

Richard Seriously though.

Brian Oh, quite seriously. Mum's the word. I wasn't here.

Richard What time is it?

Brian It's ten-past . . . oooh, I must get a little hand put on this watch. Seven. (*Fred Scuttle*) So sir, this is Fred Scuttle reporting for duty sir.

*Enter **Lisa**.*

Brian Oh, here she is then.

Lisa 'Lo, Brian.

Brian How's your head?

Lisa Not so bad, but I've lost a contact lens. Don't walk about! Have you got a torch?

Richard In the shed I think. I'll um . . .

Exit **Richard**.

Lisa Listen Brian, what we were . . . well, just now . . . I don't know what came over me.

Brian Well, Richard, presumably.

Lisa Brian!

Brian Sorry.

Lisa Honestly.

Brian Wash your mouth out, Brian. Is that it?

Lisa Oh. Yes. Thank you. The thing is I don't do things like that. This. What I just did.

She puts her lens in.

Brian Lisa; I'm see no evil, hear no evil, speak utter filth, me. But I'm very discreet.

Lisa The thing is, I'm a happily married woman.

Brian I know. And long may you remain so.

Lisa Thanks Brian.

Her head hurts.

Brian I get nervous when you've got a headache. I wonder which of us is going to pop off next.

Lisa Don't joke about it, Brian. It's a gift that can also be a burden.

Brian Oh, I can imagine.

Lisa And people do tend to make you an object of mockery.

Brian Not me.

Lisa No, not you.

Brian There's something I've been meaning to ask. Have you ever tried to . . . well, communicate with the other side?

Lisa Not for entertainment purposes, if that's what you mean.

Brian Oh no; of course not. But have you never been tempted to speak to . . . I don't know . . . to Hancock maybe. Ask him why he did something as silly as that? Tell him how much we miss him?

Lisa Well, there have been times when . . . when I think I've made contact, yes.

Brian Oh.

Lisa Three times, as a matter of fact.

Brian Mmm?

Lisa Once with Hancock, yes.

Brian Oh, sweetheart.

Lisa He came to me. I didn't call him up or anything. He came to me when they gave me my epidural.

Brian How was he?

Lisa Not very happy. He told me to fight the desire I had at the time to die. Said the afterlife wasn't all it was cracked up to be.

Brian Good Lord.

Lisa Something about long queues. Once, this was years ago, was Eric.

Brian Eric!

Lisa Eric came to me. Just after he died. I could tell it was him from a long way off because of the sock suspenders just below the hem of his toga. Now he was very happy.

Brian Oh, I'm glad; he deserves to be.

Lisa He sent a little message for Ern. I dropped him a note.

Brian What did it say?

Lisa Sorry about the early retirement. Don't let them get you on celebrity squares.

Brian Joking to the end.

Lisa And beyond really, Brian.

Brian Who else?

Lisa Well, I'm not sure about this one, but Max Miller, I think.

Brian Bless you. What did he say?

Lisa It wasn't so much what he said . . .

Brian It was the way he said it.

Lisa No, it was just his . . . presence. I think it was him.

Brian What was he wearing?

Lisa I didn't actually see him. His voice came out of the wallpaper. Lovely flowery wallpaper.

Brian Oh, that was Maxie.

Lisa I think it was.

Brian There'll never be another.

Enter **Richard**.

Lisa I've found it, thanks.

Richard Right.

Brian This woman's got a gift, you know. Well, I know you know. I'm sorry, I've got a mind like a litter tray. And I've not started drinking yet. Well, only a small gin at tea time.

Richard Would you like a drink?

Lisa Yes please.

Brian You've twisted my arm.

Doorbell. **Richard** *goes.*

Brian I know it's a gift, and I know it's something you wouldn't like to cheapen. But do you think it might be possible to speak to someone on the other side? Tell them all the things you never said.

Lisa Brian, I'm not going to call up Benny Hill.

Brian No, no. That's not what I meant.

Lisa I wouldn't want to distract him if he's making his way through limbo or something.

Brian No, I didn't mean Benny.

Enter **Nick**, *dressed as Benny Hill's Mr Chow Mein character and carrying a box of booze.*

Nick (*cod Japanese*) Ah, harrow. And a velly good evenin to you.

Brian Ohh! You look fabulous! He looks just like him, doesn't he? You look just like him.

Nick Ahh, an you fried skull. Fried skull.

Brian Oh, Fred Scuttle. That's right. That's me, sir.

Nick Preased to meet you.

Brian Pleased to meet you, sir.

Lisa Can I have that drink?

Brian You've not made much of an effort.

Richard All in good time, Brian.

Brian And there's hardly any food out.

Richard I've been busy.

Nick He slip in his cock?

Lisa What?

Nick He slip in his cock?

Lisa Um . . .

Brian I'll get the dips.

Exit **Brian**.

Nick He slip in his cock?

Richard Um . . .

Nick A *baby*!

Lisa What?

Nick Is *the baby* asleep in his cot?

Lisa Oh!

Richard Oh! Right. Is the baby asleep in his cot!

Lisa Is he asleep in his cot!

Nick Right. He asleep in his cot! Sirry iriots.

Lisa Yes. He's fast asleep.

Nick Good.

Enter **Brian**.

Brian Here we are then. Come on Richard; all hands to the deck.

Richard Oh, right.

Lisa Ooh. They look nice.

Brian Marks and Sparks.

Lisa Oh, they're very good, Marks and Spencers.

Brian They are.

Lisa They're not cheap.

Brian They're extortionate, but they're very good.

Nick You know a trubber with my wife?

Brian What's that then?

Nick Sometimes she strips and shows her bare behind up in the air.

Brian Oooh. Well.

Lisa It's a joke, Brian. He's being funny.

Brian Mmm?

Nick She strips and shows her bare behind up in the air.

Brian Oh, I see.

Lisa See?

Brian I beg your pardon, sir?

Nick She strips.

Brian She strips?

Nick And shows her bare behind . . .

Brian And shows her bare behind . . .

Nick Up in the air.

Brian Up in the air?

Nick At's right, at's what I said.

Lisa That's enough, Nick.

Nick You deaf or sumfink?

Lisa It's funny when Benny does it; when you do it it's just embarrassing.

Brian No, no no. She strips. . . ?

Nick She strips . . . strips . . . over the carpet!

Brian Trips over the carpet!

Nick And so her baby ends up in the air.

Enter **Richard** *with food.*

Brian She trips and her baby ends up in the air!

Nick That's right. That's what I said!! Strewf.

Brian Very good.

Nick Ahhhsoles.

Brian Must have taken you hours.

Lisa Well, little things please little minds.

Nick You have a good screw then?

Richard Sorry?

Nick You have a good screw, then? A good screw! For open a wine!

Lisa Oh. Ha ha ha.

Richard Oh, a corkscrew! Here.

Nick Brimey o rirey!

Brian Oh, I'm going to enjoy myself tonight. But I am very disappointed with your cozzy.

Richard All right, Brian. Just for you.

Brian I knew you'd have something up your sleeve.

Richard Two minutes.

Exit **Richard**.

Brian I knew he'd have something up his sleeve. I'll get the rest of the nibbles.

Exit **Brian**.

Lisa All right, babe? How was the car today?

Nick Oh, it had a great time. Particularly enjoyed its push-start across the playground by the fourth-form netball team.

Lisa So did you, probably. Max had a nice day. Ate a whole banana. And he said another word, and he's only nine months. He said Dada. It was very clear. Dada. It's a pity you weren't there; I could have pointed at you. That's four words he's got now; Muma, More, Dada and Yoplait. And his pooh was quite solid today; quite grown up. Of course, on the way to the shops his fan belt broke and I had to call out the RAC, but other than that. . . .

Pause.

Nick Pardon?

Lisa 'Pardon?'

Enter **Brian** *with, amongst other things, a large trifle.*

Brian Here we are then; and I'll tell you this for nothing. You don't get one of these out of a packet.

Lisa Ooh lovely, Brian.

Richard (*off*) Brian!

Brian What?

Richard (*off*) Introduce me.

Brian Oh, right. Ladies and gentlemen, here he is, the lad himself . . . Benny Hill.

Richard *enters. Grey wig, big smile, pink shirt and tie, dreadful check jacket.*

Brian Oh, perfect.

Lisa Oh my God.

Brian That is brilliant.

Nick Very good, mate.

Brian You're the spitting image.

Richard I hope not.

Nick The wig is brilliant.

Brian Perfect.

Nick Where did you get it?

Richard Oxfam.

Nick Imagine; someone actually wore that. I mean, if that's the sort of hair you haven't got any more it's good riddance, surely.

Lisa Where did you get that jacket!

Richard Well . . .

Nick Institute for the Blind, I should think.

Lisa It's really horrible.

Richard Well, it's um . . .

Nick Gruesome.

Richard It's um . . .

Brian Mine as a matter of fact.

Richard It's Brian's.

Lisa It's a lovely colour.

Brian Oh, it's years old. I thought you were up to something. Who wants another drink?

Nick Me.

Lisa Me, please.

Brian *pours.*

Nick Of course, you couldn't actually wear a jacket like that on TV you know; it'd cause linear strobing.

Brian I'll have you know I looked very dapper in that, once upon a time.

Nick *tastes his wine.*

Nick Ah, rubbery.

Brian Shouldn't be; do you want another glass?

Nick No, it's rubbery. A wine is rubbery!

Brian Oh. Sirry Iriot. Let's have a sneaky toast before the mob arrive. To Benny.

Nick We'll miss you, mate.

Richard To Benny.

Lisa Rest in peace.

They sit.

Nick (*quietly, sadly*) Dee dee dee dee dee diddle diddle dee dee diddle diddle dee diddle diddly dum! Dee dee dee . . .

All (*joining in separately*) . . . Dee dee diddle diddle dee dee diddle diddle dee diddle diddly dum!

Eleanor *enters.*

All except Eleanor Dee diddle dum diddle dum diddle dum diddle diddle dum dum diddle dum diddle dum diddle diddle dum! Diddle diddle diddle! Diddle diddle dum! Diddle de dum dum!

Nick Rom pom tiddle tiddle rom pom oom pom . . .

All except Eleanor Rom pom tiddle tiddle rom pom oom pom . . .

Brian Pom pom pom pom!

Lisa Rom pom pom pom!

Richard Pom pom pom pom pom!!! Hello, Ellie.

Eleanor I thought for a moment I had the wrong house. But no, right house. Wrong life.

Brian Now put a smile on your face; we're throwing a party here.

Eleanor I think I'd rather walk into a party thrown by. . . .

Brian Who?

Eleanor No one.

Richard Who?

Nick Who?

Eleanor I was going to say Denis Nillson, but you'd think I was a horrible person, so I didn't.

Nick *laughs a lot. Stops.*

Nick Well, I think it's funny.

Eleanor That's because you *are* . . .

Eleanor/Lisa . . . a horrible person.

Richard I thought you had a class.

Eleanor No one turned up.

Lisa What are you teaching?

Eleanor Classroom skills. One of them sent a note. Says he's a grown adult and doesn't like being screamed at for not doing his homework. Give me a drink. No one else here yet?

Brian Oh, it's early yet. Have you got a costume?

Eleanor Have I, fuck. Richard, could I have a word?

Nick I was hoping you'd come as a Hill's Angel.

Lisa Nick.

Eleanor Richard?

Richard Ellie, it's a party. Have a drink.

Brian Stuff a cushion up your cardy and be Bella Emberg.

Eleanor Please, Richard.

Richard Enjoy yourself.

Nick Richard. (*Sings quietly.*) Will you miss me tonight . . .

Brian Ohh . . .

Lisa Oh, yes.

Richard No.

Nick Go on.

Richard Oh, all right.

Eleanor Richard . . .

Richard *becomes his own approximation of Eric Morcambe.*

Richard (*sings*) Will you miss me tonight . . .

Nick Oh, right.

Richard (*sings*) When I'm home? Will your love be the same . . .

Nick *becomes Ernie Wise.*

Nick What are you doing?

Richard Eh?

Nick What are you doing?

Richard Ah, well, I've found something out. I don't need you. You're not a nasset any more, to me. I'm going to do it all by myself. Sing, by myself. I'm going to be a big star.

Nick But you're not doing it right.

Richard Aren't I?

Nick No; you can't be a star on your own.

Richard Oh.

Nick You've got to have backing.

Richard Have you?

Nick Sure. Now I'm a group.

Richard No.

Nick Yeh.

Richard All by yourself?

Nick No, no no no. There's Dick, Sid, and me.

Richard Oh.

Nick Come on.

Brian Oh, you daft buggers.

Nick Now Dick, he's a boomer.

Brian Boom.

Richard That was good.

Nick And Sid, he's an oo-er.

Richard Is he?

Nick Sid; give him an oo-er.

Lisa OooOooOooh.

Richard That's clever that. That's good that.

Nick And me, I'm a ya-ta-ta-ta-er.

Richard Oh, this is great.

Nick We'll make you into a big star.

Richard I'm glad you came.

Nick Right. Here we go fellers . . . a one, two . . .

Brian Boom!

Lisa Oooh!

Richard Ya ta ta ta!

(*Repeat.*)

Nick (*sings*) Will you miss me tonight, when I'm gone? Will your love be the same from now on . . .

Richard Ya ta . . . ta . . . ta . . . Ya . . . No, wait, no wait a minute boys. No, what's happening . . . Hold it lads. What's happening is I'm ya ta ta ta- ing, you see. I'm ya ta ta ta-ing instead of Miss-Me-Tonight-ing.

Nick Oh well, perhaps I shouldn't have started it.

Richard Oh.

Nick We'll let Sid start it.

Richard Good. That's good.

Nick OK, Sid.

Lisa And one, two . . .

Brian Boom!

Richard Oooh!

Nick Ya ta ta ta!

Lisa Will you miss me tonight, when I'm gone? Will your love be the same from now on . . .

Richard Ooh, no. No, just a . . . hold it boys, you see what's happening . . .

Brian Boom diddy boom diddy boom de boom boom boom . . .

Richard Dick. Dick. Dick. Dick. Dick! He's away, Dick is, isn't he? No, you see what's happening is I'm Oooh-ing now. I've ya ta ta ta-ed, I've Oooh-ed . . . I've only got a boom to go.

Nick Perhaps Sid shouldn't have started it.

Richard Well, I didn't want to say anything when you suggested that . . .

Nick Would you like to start it?

Richard Well, if you insist.

Nick Well, all right.

Richard If it'll make it any easier for you. Yes. Well now, this is what happens boys, it's . . . Boom! Oooh! Ya ta ta ta! Boom! Oooh! Ya ta ta ta! . . .

(*Repeat.*)

Others (*sing*) Will you miss me tonight, when I'm gone? Will your love be the same from now on . . .

Richard It's tough at the top, isn't it?

They applaud themselves. **Ellie** *remains stoney-faced.*

Brian Oh, yes.

Lisa Sid Green and Dick Hills.

Brian The best.

Richard Probably the best sketch ever written.

Nick Oh no.

Richard No?

Nick No I beg to differ. The best sketch ever . . .

Brian With the exception of 'Who's On Next?'

Nick Yes, right, well, with the exception of 'Who's On Next?' . . .

Brian Because that's American.

Richard The best British sketch . . .

Lisa Dead Parrot?

Nick No no no no.

Richard What?

Brian Which one?

Nick *gets up.*

Nick Hey! Are you putting it around that I'm barmy?

Brian Oh . . . yes!

Richard Good heavens, no.

Lisa Jimmy James.

Brian Oh, brilliant.

Nick Is it him then?

Richard I don't know. Is it you that's putting it around that he's barmy?

Brian I don't want any.

Richard He doesn't want any.

They laugh.

Nick Great stuff.

Lisa The one and only.

Brian Jimmy James.

Eleanor I wouldn't be so bewildered by your love for dead comedians if when they were alive you actually laughed at them.

Brian Of course we laugh at them.

Eleanor He doesn't. I've watched him watching them and he doesn't laugh.

Richard Of course I laugh.

Eleanor You might think you do but you don't.

Richard I do.

Eleanor The odd wry smile is not laughter. The occasional meaningful nod is not laughter. A muttered 'very good' or 'oh, excellent', is not laughter. Appreciation it may be and Lord knows you sit there appreciating 'til the cows come home, but laugh you do not!

Richard Ignore her.

Brian What's the time?

Nick It's twenty-past . . . ooh, I must get a little hand put on this watch. Eight.

Brian They should have started arriving by now, you know.

Eleanor If they're dressed like you four they've probably all been arrested.

Nick When's Henry coming?

Brian Oh well, he's performing you see. Not until after eleven.

Nick Oh well, they'll be here by then.

Brian Oh yes, they'll all be here by then.

Lisa Actually, I'm not sure they will, not actually.

Brian What do you mean?

Eleanor She's got a massive migraine; there's been a pile-up on the M25 and the Northern line's caught fire.

Lisa Well actually I have got a bit of a headache but that's not it. We had a phone call late this afternoon. From Les Rollins. He said he wasn't going to come.

Brian Oh well, good. I'm glad.

Lisa He said he was having a few people round. He said would we like to come. I said no, of course not; we're having a do at Richard's. Best of British, he said, and put the phone down.

Brian He did what?

Nick Why didn't you tell us?

Lisa I was hoping they might turn up.

Brian A few people round? How many people?

Lisa I don't know.

Richard I shouldn't think many.

Brian I'm the last to wish ill on anyone, but I sometimes wish Les Rollins had died of that heart attack.

Nick No one'll go.

Richard Roger maybe; he and Les seem thick as thieves, but I shouldn't think he'd have the nerve to phone round the entire society. I mean he didn't phone here. I mean, he's not very popular.

Lisa He's been getting more popular.

Nick Rumour has it someone recently touched him with a barge pole.

Richard And it's goodnight from me.

Nick And goodnight from him.

Brian How dare he! How dare he do this!

Richard Calm down, Brian. He may have phoned round, but that doesn't mean anyone's going to choose to go round his place.

Nick Well, not everyone.

Richard Some maybe.

Nick One or two. I bet they bloody will, you know.

Richard Toby wouldn't.

Nick Toby won't.

Lisa He rang to see if you were.

Brian Oh no! It's not on. This society has a constitution. Unwritten maybe, but a constitution all the same.

Eleanor Oh for Christ's sake; it's good riddance to the anoraks, surely? We'll be able to get up and down the hall to the front door without suffocating.

Nick I remember where that second cashcard went now. I gave it to Rollins to pay the printers.

Eleanor Richard. Could you give me a hand in the kitchen?

Richard Brian, the night is young. Most of them'll turn up.

Brian Well they'd better, or I'm resigning.

Eleanor If they don't, you won't have to.

Richard Come on, cheer up.

Eleanor Richard?

Richard Hey! I've been to Africa, you know.

Nick Right, come on, Brian. Have you?

Richard Yeh. They gave me a present.

Nick What did they give you?

Richard Two man-eating lions.

Nick Real lions?

Richard Yeh.

Nick Did you fetch them to England?

Richard Yeh.

Nick Where'd you keep them?

Richard In this box.

Nick Are they in there now?

Richard Yes.

Nick I thought I heard a rustling. Go and get two cups of coffee. One with strychnine in.

Richard Are you telling him about the lions?

Nick Oh, he's got two lions in this box.

Brian How much are they?

Richard They gave me a giraffe as well.

Nick Where do you keep the giraffe?

Richard In the box.

Nick Get on the phone. I'll keep him talking.

Richard Hey.

Nick What?

Richard I've been to India as well.

Nick I bet the Indians gave you a present.

Richard Yeh.

Nick What did they give you?

Richard An elephant.

Nick Male or female?

Richard No, an elephant. I brought it home with me, you know.

Nick The elephant?

Richard Yeh.

Nick I hardly like to ask. I've got an idea, like. Where d'you keep it, in the box?

Richard Don't be silly; you couldn't get an elephant in there.

Brian You could ask the giraffe to move over a bit.

Richard No, no. I keep the elephant in a cage.

Nick He keeps it in a cage, you silly thing. Where do you keep the cage?

Richard/Nick In the box.

They laugh. They toast.

Richard Jimmy James.

Nick/Lisa/Brian Jimmy James.

Richard Don't smile; you might crack your face.

Eleanor If I've heard this stuff once. . . .

Nick (*Max Miller*) I've got one for you, lady. But if I crack this joke, don't laugh, 'cos if you laugh the manager'll know it's rude. So, I knocked on the door of this boarding house, and a lady came to the door . . .

Lisa *smiles.* **Richard** *and* **Brian** *laugh.* **Eleanor** *doesn't.*

Nick No, don't! Shh. She was a nice lady . . . a little bit and some more, a not quite so much, and then a perhaps . . . no, keep it down. You'll get me into trouble. I said could you accommodate me? She said I'm sorry, I'm full up. I said surely you could squeeze me in your little back room. She said I could, but I haven't got time now. No, shush. Shush. You'll get me arrested. Take a good look lady . . .

Brian/Nick/Richard There'll never be another.

Richard My father used to do Max Miller.

Brian Oh, really?

Richard Once a year, on boxing day, between cold turkey for lunch and curried turkey for supper, he'd disappear and come downstairs dressed in some old curtains and he'd launch into

Max Miller. Us kids'd be on the carpet; we'd be rolling around. My mother pretending to be shocked. He did a whole routine. Learnt it off a record. It was a big treat for us kids, seeing him muck about like that. Laughing.

Eleanor First time I've ever heard you remember your father fondly.

Richard It's about the only time I can remember him.

Nick I remember him. Scared the life out of me.

Richard Boxing day's all I remember.

Eleanor He's got a lot to answer for, your father.

Richard I don't think he had any influence on me at all.

Eleanor Ha.

Richard What do you mean Ha?

Eleanor He was a consultant obstetrician. You're a consultant obstetrician. Was that a coincidence?

Richard He'd have been happy whatever I chose.

Eleanor Happy! Your father?

Richard He didn't push me into anything.

Eleanor Some fathers push, some fathers suck. Yours sucked.

Richard Please, Eleanor.

Eleanor He treated your mother like dirt. Virtually ignored her for thirty years then discarded her like a used car, because he fancied a newer model.

Richard How do you know?

Eleanor Because she told me. When we did that big jigsaw of Mevagissy harbour together. By the time we'd done the sky, I knew all about your father.

Richard He's got nothing to do with it.

Eleanor We got quite close before she died. She said you were more like him than you ever thought you were.

Richard I'm nothing like him.

Nick There'll never be another!

Brian Oh, there'll never be another! There was of course.

Nick What?

Brian A pretender. Not as good as The Cheeky Chappie, but when it comes to playing an audience, almost as great as Max.

Nick Doddy?

Brian Well yes of course, but no . . . my favourite. My absolute favourite. Richard knows.

Richard Frankie.

Brian Frankie.

Nick Oh well, Frankie!

Lisa Oh yes.

Nick I should say so; yes missus.

Richard No, don't. You mustn't.

Lisa Now apparently, he was a little bit psychic.

Brian Go on Nick; do him for me.

Nick No, well, what did you expect, class? You've come to the wrong place, then. On what they're paying me you're lucky to get the suit. Now, before we start this little eisteddfod, I'm going to make a little appeal. It's all right, it's not for money; you've been robbed as it is. No, don't titter. Titter ye not! Well if you must, then for gawdsake all get them out at the same time. Go on missus; get your titters out!

Brian Oh, he's the best.

Richard The best. We went to see Frankie when we were what?

Nick We were nineteen-years-old.

Richard At the Palladium. My father was given tickets by one of the Beverly Sisters who had an ectopic pregnancy, but he couldn't go.

Nick That's what started it for me really, that night.

Richard It was a great night. No don't!

Nick Oh, please yourselves. Best night of my life.

Lisa Oh, thank you very much.

Brian Ooh; hark at her, sat sitting there.

Nick All fur coat and no knickers.

Lisa Charming, I'm sure.

Nick I'm not saying she's a loose woman.

Brian No?

Nick But they'll have to bury her in a Y shaped coffin.

Laughter.

Brian Well, I think it's Ellie's turn.

Eleanor I haven't got a turn.

Nick Come on, Ellie.

Brian Go on Ellie; don't be a partypooper; tell us a joke.

Richard She can't tell jokes.

Eleanor Yes I can.

Richard You don't know any jokes.

Eleanor I know a joke. I overheard a joke in a pub once.

Richard Bet you can't remember it.

Lisa Go on, Ellie.

Eleanor A man took his wife to the doctor. The doctor examined her and told the man she either had alzheimer's disease or aids. The man said, which? The doctor said it's impossible to tell. The man said; how can I find out? The doctor said put her in the car, drive her out into the woods about four or five miles, drop her off . . . and if she finds her way back, don't fuck her.

A pause. **Nick** *laughs, strangles.*

Eleanor If you don't touch me soon. Not sexually, necessarily, not by appointment. But just casually, accidentally even . . . a simple touch. If you can no longer even touch me, I think I shall go mad.

Brian You know, I don't dislike this fabric.

Nick No, missus. Don't.

Lisa Excuse me.

Brian What's wrong?

Lisa I'm feeling a bit peculiar.

Brian Oh, sweetheart. Can I help?

Nick (*Frankie*) No, take no notice; she's a peculiar woman.

Eleanor Lisa?

Nick No, don't. Don't encourage her.

Eleanor You've gone very pale.

Nick Poor soul.

Eleanor She looks awful.

Nick No, don't.

Lisa Frankie?

Nick It's cruel.

Lisa Frankie?

Nick Don't mock the afflicted.

Lisa *faints.*

Brian Oh dear.

Eleanor Lisa?

Richard *becomes a doctor*, **Eleanor** *and* **Brian** *gather round.*

Eleanor Is she all right?

Richard She's just fainted, I think. Has she been ill?

Nick Bit run down.

Richard Lisa?

Lisa Ooh.

Brian Ah.

Eleanor All right, Lisa?

Brian She's all right. She's back.

Lisa Sorry.

Richard Careful. Don't get up.

Lisa Don't want to spoil the party.

Brian You just sit there for a bit.

Lisa Sorry. Ellie. I'm really sorry.

Eleanor What for?

Lisa I am, really.

Richard You should lie down.

Lisa I'm really sorry.

Richard Let's get you upstairs.

Richard *carries her out.*

Brian Poor thing.

Nick She'll be all right.

Eleanor Has she seen anyone about those headaches.

Nick Oh yes. She errs on the safe side. Had a load of tests, year before last, all OK. Even had a brain scan. They didn't find anything. Boom boom.

Brian Oh, yes. Ha.

Eleanor Aren't you in the least concerned?

Nick She's highly strung, that's all. Personally I'd string her a bit higher.

Eleanor Nick!

Nick Well, you don't have to live with it. I'm the one it's making ill.

Richard *returns.*

Richard She's on our bed.

Pause.

Brian What's the time?

Richard It's ten past . . . ooh . . .

Eleanor Please. Don't.

Richard . . . I haven't got a watch on.

Nick It's twenty-five past nine.

Brian They're not coming, are they?

Eleanor That's right Brian; look on the bright side.

The lights fade.

Scene Two

The same. Two hours later. They've all been drinking. **Brian** *is deeply unhappy.* **Eleanor** *brooding.* **Richard** *numb.* **Nick** *merry but quiet.*

Richard What have you achieved? You contributed absolutely nothing to this life. A waste of time you being here at all.

Brian I know.

Nick Shh.

Richard No plaque for you in Westminster Abbey; all you can expect is a few daffodils in a jamjar. Cor, dear oh dear . . .

Nick Hancock.

Brian Hancock.

Nick Ray Galton, Alan Simpson.

Richard No one'll even notice you're not here. After about a year afterwards somebody might say down the pub; 'Where's old Hancock? I haven't seen him around lately.' 'Oh, he's dead you know.' 'Oh, is he?' A right raison d'etre that is!

Nick That's right. And they wrote that . . .

Richard That was the last television script they wrote him.

Nick Was it?

Richard The last one.

Nick That's . . . wierd.

Lisa *enters.*

Lisa Hello.

Brian Oh, there she is.

Eleanor Are you feeling better?

Lisa I fell asleep.

Eleanor How do you feel?

Lisa Oh, much better. Just a bit of a headache.

Nick Les Rollins' flat burned to the ground with no survivors.

Eleanor Leave her alone.

Brian Don't try and cheer me up Nick, I'm not in the mood.

Lisa I'm sorry to be a nuisance. It's the breast feeding, I think. I'm on iron tablets, but apparently they don't dissolve anyway. Oh well. Hello again.

Brian Hello.

Richard Hello.

Lisa No one else came then?

Eleanor Oh yes, they all came. But they were wearing sensible clothes so we didn't let them in.

Richard Look on the bright side Brian. In twenty minutes' time you'll have Henry McGee all to yourself.

Eleanor The bright side presumably being the twenty minutes.

Brian I should think Henry's a man of his word.

Richard One of the gentlemen of the profession I should think.

Brian And he'll be more at ease in a small gathering.

Richard That's right.

Nick That's right.

Brian Before he does arrive, there is something I wanted to say. If I don't say it now I never will. So, here goes. This might come as a bit of a shock to you all, coming out of the blue.

Eleanor What's wrong?

Brian Oh, nothing's wrong. I just wanted to say a few words about Benny. Now over the years I've met a number of people who've been acquainted with one or other of the girls that Benny was obliged to work with, and I was always gratified to learn, indeed the girls were often at pains to stress, that at all times he behaved like a perfect gentleman. That for all the necessarily salacious material that they performed with him, there was never, ever, a hint of impropriety. Well, Benny's gone now, and of course the press are going to have a field day. Which is sad because he was always an intensely private man. A solitary, and many believe, celibate man. Well, wherever he is, he'll have to forgive me for this, but I believe otherwise. I believe Benny was gay.

Nick Bloody hell.

Lisa You mean queer?

Brian He was a homosexual, yes. No funny comments please, Ellie.

Eleanor I'm speechless.

Brian Don't mock, because after you've heard what I'm going to say you might wish you hadn't.

Eleanor Sorry, Brian.

Brian Benny was gay. So, I believe, are many other great comedians. Including, and this is not a thing I'd say in public because it's not a thing he's chosen to make public himself, including Frankie Howerd.

Eleanor My world is shattered.

Ellie *silenced by a look from* **Brian**.

Brian Frankie is gay. Deep breath. And so am I.

Pause.

Lisa What?

Brian Gay.

Long pause.

Brian There. You see. I knew you'd be speechless.

Eleanor *opens her mouth and closes it.*

Richard Well. . . .

Lisa Well, well, well.

Nick *sniggers. Turns away.*

Brian You're all good friends. Good friends. I hope it won't make any difference.

Eleanor Of course it won't.

Richard Thanks for sharing it with us.

Brian I feel quite light-headed. It's as if a great weight's been lifted off my mind.

Nick Brian. . . ?

Eleanor Nick.

Brian What?

Nick Nothing.

He turns away again. His shoulders heave.

Eleanor How long have you known, Brian?

Brian Well to be honest, I've had my suspicions for quite some time. Mum was always on at me to get a girlfriend. Then, I shouldn't tell you this, but a had a little encounter in the post room at work with a despatch rider and that clinched it really. So I took a deep breath and I told mum. I said mum, I'm gay. She said Brian, you're not. You're all right. I didn't want to worry her, so I just let it lie.

Lisa You're not really, are you? Queer?

Eleanor Lisa.

Lisa Well, I know he's camp as a row of tents. We've always known that . . .

Richard Lisa . . .

Lisa But I never realised you were actually queer.

Richard I think the word is gay.

Lisa Same difference.

Brian You're all a bit shocked; I know; I quite understand.

Richard Well, I think it's great news. I think we should drink on it.

Eleanor Absolutely. To Brian's Coming Out.

Brian Oh, I suppose so. I suppose it is, yes. Out of the closet. I only wish I'd known where I was all these years.

Eleanor To Brian.

Richard To Brian.

Nick To Brian.

Eleanor Our gay friend.

Brian Oh, and look; I'm going to celebrate in style.

Takes a slip of paper out of his wallet.

Eleanor What is it?

Brian A ticket to Amsterdam.

Nick Amsterdam?

Richard What are you going to do in Amsterdam?

Eleanor Richard.

Richard Oh.

Brian I realise some of you . . . that there has to be some adjustment.

Lisa Don't look at me. I'm not homosemitic.

Nick Phobic.

Lisa Phobic. I'm just a bit surprised.

Nick You've known him for years. How could you be surprised?

Lisa Well, we're all surprised aren't we? Aren't we?

Nick I thought you were supposed to be clairvoyant.

Lisa I don't know what you're angry at me for.

Nick You wouldn't know if Christmas was coming.

Lisa Well if he didn't know he was queer, how the bloody hell am I supposed to know; I'm not psychic! Well, I am a little bit, but not like that!

Nick Oh, shut up.

Lisa I'm not Ellie, Nick. Don't tell me to shut up in front of other people.

Nick Then stop talking bollocks.

Richard Steady on, Nick. She's not feeling well.

Lisa Excuse me.

Lisa *exits.*

Eleanor What's the matter with you, Nick?

Nick I have to live with her.

Eleanor You chose to live with her.

Nick Whose side are you on?

Eleanor I'm not on anyone's . . . hers!

Nick You take the piss out of her all evening and all of a sudden I'm supposed to sit here while she prattles on . . .

Richard Nick. You're out of order, mate.

Nick It's her who's out of order! You don't know the fucking half of it either so mind your own sodding business.

Brian Look, did I start this? I hope I didn't start this.

Eleanor You didn't start anything. Nick; you're pissed.

Nick So would you be.

Brian I need a breath of fresh air.

Eleanor Brian; it's not your fault.

Brian Once round the block. I won't be long.

Eleanor I'll come with you.

Brian No. It is my fault. Bad timing.

Exit **Brian**

Eleanor What is wrong with you two?

Richard I didn't say a word.

Eleanor That was a big step for Brian.

Nick Oh come on Ellie; I've never met a bigger pooftah.

Eleanor It's taken him years to do what he did tonight. It took a lot of courage. More courage than you two could muster put together.

Richard Why am I involved in this all of a sudden?

Eleanor Because you're vile. Both of you. All of you. If it's something you can't snigger at, you run a mile.

Richard What are you talking about?

Eleanor The difference between us.

Eleanor *exits, following* **Lisa** *upstairs.*

Nick Sorry.

Richard That's all right mate. I don't know what's going on.

Nick It's been getting worse and worse lately; I'm really tensed up, you know? Getting married was a fucking mistake. You should have talked me out of it when I begged you to.

Richard It's often hard just after your first child; so I've heard.

Nick Yes, well that hasn't helped.

Richard Oh come on Nick; you must be happy about the kid. You always wanted kids.

Nick Are we good friends, Richard?

Richard I hope so.

Nick Because if we're not, I haven't got any.

Richard Yes; we're friends.

Nick I know we go back a long way, but it's not always the same thing, is it? Things change.

Richard If there's something you want to say Nick, say it.

Nick Well yes, there is. Lisa doesn't know this. Couple of years ago I got a bit worried about it all. We'd been trying so long, and she'd started going on about IVF. So I didn't tell her but I went to a clinic in Fulham. Private place, very nice, nice people.

Pause.

Richard Mmm.

Nick Long and short of it is . . . I had some tests done.

Richard I see.

Nick I'm telling you this in confidence.

Richard Sure.

Nick They actually count the sperm.

Richard Oh, yes.

Nick How many normal, how many swimming. Two hundred and fifty million sperms per mil. of come.

Richard That was your count?

Nick No, that's the average.

Richard I know.

Nick Mine was lower. Mine was nil. Azoo . . . whatsit.

Richard Spermia.

Nick Right. I didn't tell Lisa. Bit of a shock. Three months later she gave me a bigger one.

Richard Well, there you go. The labs sometimes botch these things. Put the wrong time on the dish; the slide gets left on the bench . . .

Nick That's what I thought, so I went to another clinic. Had it done again.

Richard And?

Nick It's not my kid.

Richard You don't know that.

Nick It's not my kid.

Richard Does Lisa know?

Nick She doesn't know it's not.

Richard You haven't told her?

Nick She hasn't told me. I know she knows it might not be, but she doesn't know I know it's not.

Richard You mean it *might* not be.

Nick The point is she thinks I think it definitely is and I know it definitely isn't.

Richard Why haven't you said anything?

Nick I thought I could cope. I thought I could, but I can't. I hate being with her. I hate her voice. I hate her face. And I hate the kid. What do you think I should do?

Enter **Ellie**.

Eleanor Come on in.

Enter **Lisa**.

Eleanor Nick. Apologise to your wife.

Richard He's very sorry.

Eleanor Not you. Him.

Lisa Never mind.

Eleanor I mean it. I will not have someone treated like that in my house.

Richard Our house.

Eleanor Don't push your luck. Well?

Nick I'm very sorry.

Eleanor Thank you.

Nick I'm mortally ashamed of myself.

Lisa It's all right.

Nick I am unfit to suck the sweat from your maternity bra strap and I humbly beg . . .

Eleanor Shut up.

Enter **Brian**.

Brian Am I still welcome?

Eleanor Oh Brian.

Richard Brian.

Eleanor Come in and sit down.

Brian Only I got as far as the King's Head and I realised, he should be here any minute. Henry.

Lisa Brian, certain people seem to forget that I was in the business myself for a short time during which I rubbed shoulders with a number of q . . . homosexuals. And quite a few queens. And you can take it from me that not all the queens were homosexuals or all the homosexuals queens. So I never judge from appearances, and Brian, I am certainly not homophobic.

Eleanor Lisa, we know.

Richard We know.

Lisa Good. He is.

Nick No I'm not.

Lisa Yes you are. He is.

Nick Brian . . .

Lisa Don't deny it just for Brian's sake.

Richard Lisa.

Lisa John Inman came on the telly the other night; he turned over and watched a documentary about Haringay Council.

Nick Why do you talk such absolute bollocks?

Lisa Why do you pretend to be everybody's friend when you're always criticising them behind their backs?

Nick When did I ever. . . ?

Lisa Richard won't lend me his car and Brian's an old queen and Eleanor's a pain in the . . .

Nick Lisa! Look, I never . . .

Richard Why don't we all just . . .

Lisa That's what you said.

Nick Passing comments. Lighthearted banter.

Lisa Vitriol.

Eleanor Listen. If I may be a pain in the arse just for one moment. I wasn't looking forward to this evening. I've got problems of my own. Well, of Richard's. Well, Richard, basically.

Richard Don't call me Richard.

Eleanor Sorry Trevor.

Nick Trevor?

Eleanor I'm not preserving this thin veneer of civilised behaviour over the barren god-awful mess that is my marriage so that you lot can act like the Borgias, so cheer up or go home!

Lisa Sorry.

Brian We couldn't go yet Ellie. Henry'll be here any minute.

Eleanor You see? There is always something to look forward to.

Telephone rings.

Eleanor Would you mind answering that, Philip?

Lisa Philip?

Nick Who's Trevor?

Richard Seven three eight four. Hello Toby. Are you? Good. No, we're having a great time here too. Has he? I see. Yes, we were wondering. Did he? Has he? Yeh. I don't think I can Toby, not really. Well, actually Toby, it's a loyalty thing. Well, I don't suppose you would.

Puts phone down.

Brian He's gone there, hasn't he?

Richard Rollins told Henry McGee there'd been a change of venue. Turned up with Ray Cooney apparently. And June Whitfield.

Brian Well, that's it then; I resign.

Nick He asked you over, did he?

Richard Oh well, we're all welcome to go over.

Pause.

Brian Well I'm not.

Nick Oh, I'm not.

Richard I said I wasn't.

Lisa When you meet a famous person, it's never as exciting as you'd think. They just look the same but smaller. I bet they're all dead small.

Nick It doesn't matter what bloody size they are, does it?

Lisa You know what my mother once said to Jimmy Clitheroe? She was in Dick Whittington with Jimmy Clitheroe, this is true, and he came up to her and he said 'What would you say to a little fuck?' and she said . . .

All 'Piss off, little fuck.'

Lisa I told you that then?

Nick She made it up.

Lisa It's true.

Nick She more likely said; 'Yes, please'.

Lisa She's six-foot, my mum.

Nick Probably explains why you're four-foot ten.

Lisa Don't start.

Nick Well I've heard stranger theories about your genetic history.

Lisa Nick, please.

Nick I mean you've said it yourself; your mother wasn't exactly choosy, was she?

Lisa I never said that.

Eleanor Leave her alone.

Nick Tell them your theory.

Lisa I haven't got a theory.

Nick Go on, tell them your theory.

Eleanor Nick!

Nick You may not realise it but we are looking at the illegitimate daughter of . . .

Lisa Nick! There are certain things shared between a man and wife that are personal things. Things other people wouldn't be interested in anyway.

Richard Right.

Brian Absolutely.

Lisa All right?

Nick Right.

Pause.

Richard Of who?

Nick Sid James.

Richard/Brian Sid James!

Lisa I only said it once! It was just a thought! It was only something I thought once!

Nick Different woman every film apparently. Lunchtimes, in his caravan.

Richard Of course; *Carry on, Matron.*

Brian Seriously?

Lisa There was a couple of photos, that's all, and Nick said . . .

Nick You said . . .

Lisa I didn't say it. I said she used to speak very fondly of him. You're the one who got out Halliwell's Film Guide and worked out the dates.

Nick Dates work out perfectly.

Lisa I never said . . .

Nick I mean there is a resemblance, you have to admit it.

Lisa Nick! It's not true.

Pause.

Lisa It's not true.

Nick (*Sid's laugh*) Yuk yuk yuk yuk yuk.

Lisa Shut up!

Brian Even if it was true . . .

Eleanor Brian.

Richard Nothing to be ashamed of, quite the contrary.

Lisa Please, Richard.

Richard No, I mean seriously; what's on your birth certificate?

Eleanor Richard! Mind your own business.

Richard Well he was a notorious womaniser. Propositioned every woman he met.

Eleanor How would you know?

Nick Takes one to know one, eh mate?

Eleanor Well he wouldn't know one; he's been celibate for a year and a half.

Lisa Hu!

Richard Could we keep our private lives private?

Eleanor Pardon?

Richard Could we just wait . . .

Eleanor Not you; her.

Richard All I said was . . .

Eleanor I heard what you said; what did she say?

Lisa I didn't say anything.

Eleanor You said 'Hu!'.

Lisa No I didn't.

Eleanor Yes you did. You said 'Hu!'.

Lisa No, I didn't say 'Hu!', I said 'Ahah!'

Eleanor So I say Richard's celibate and you say 'Ahah!'?

Lisa Mmm?

Eleanor So what does that mean? 'Ahah!'

Lisa Well, it explains why you two aren't getting on so I said 'Ahah!', meaning now we know why Ellie's in such a foul . . . well, why she's acting a bit . . . well, why she's, I mean why you . . . aren't very happy at the moment.

Eleanor But you didn't say 'Ahah!', you said 'Hu!'

Lisa Well, I meant 'Ahah!'.

Eleanor (*to* **Richard**) Are you screwing someone else?

Pause.

Brian Well, I think it's time for Uncle Brian to wend his weary way . . .

Richard Are you off, Bri?

Eleanor Sit down, Brian. Are you screwing someone else?

Richard Could we talk about this later?

Eleanor Oh, I should think so. We'll talk about it later just as soon as we've finished talking about it right now. Lisa.

Lisa Mmmm?

Eleanor Has my husband told you he's screwing someone else?

Lisa I don't want to get involved in this.

Eleanor You said 'Hu!'. Which means he's told you something I don't know. Which means that you must know him a damn bloody sight more. . . .

Long pause.

Brian Well . . .

Eleanor Sit down, Brian. If at this late stage in your life you intend to enter the sexual arena, I think you'd better stay and watch this.

Lisa Take me home, please? Nick?

Eleanor Don't think about standing up Lisa, because you'd never make it to the door.

Richard Ellie.

Eleanor You sat with me on those horrible chairs in Miriam's room and you said you didn't want to be touched. You said it was nothing to do with me. You said you felt No Desire. You sounded like Christ on the cross. So in spite of my desperation I have been patient, in spite of my bewilderment I have been understanding, in spite of my feeling of utter abandonment . . . I've been hanging on in there. Trying to help you come through this terrible thing. And all this time . . . How many times? Don't tell me; I don't care. All this time you've been screwing the illegitimate daughter of Sid James. I'm beginning to see the resemblance.

Richard I think we should let these people go home.

Lisa *gets up, goes to her bag, takes aspirin.*

Lisa I really have got a really bad headache now.

Eleanor Maybe someone's going to die.

Lisa I think it's a migraine.

Eleanor Probably you, then.

Lisa Look, it's not true! You've got hold of completely the wrong end of the stick. It's not true, is it Richard?

Long pause.

Lisa You sod. Ellie, it wasn't an affair or anything. It was completely meaningless.

Eleanor *strides towards* **Lisa**. **Nick** *catches her arm.*

Nick Ellie. No. Don't. Leave her alone.

Nick *rises and goes to* **Lisa**.

Lisa It was his idea, I didn't even fancy him. He said you only live once. He said he's never wanted anyone like he wanted me. He said I was . . .

Nick What?

Lisa Beautiful.

Nick *hits her very hard in the face with one of the mini custard pies.*

Eleanor Not to mention dignified.

Brian Oh dear oh dear.

Richard Steady on, mate . . .

Nick What!?

Richard Nick . . .

Nick What?! I'm sorry, did you speak? You got something to say to me?

Richard Nick, it was nothing.

Lisa It was nothing to do with you.

Eleanor Nothing to what?

Nick *throws lots of food at* **Richard**.

Nick You disloyal, lying, two-faced fucking shit-head.

Richard For Christ's sake mate.

Nick Don't mate me, you toad. You fucking parasite.

Eleanor Mind the furniture, Nick.

Lisa It was purely physical, Ellie. Completely mindless.

Eleanor Well in your case it would have to be.

Lisa Men need a certain amount of sex Ellie; if they can't get it at home . . .

Eleanor *goes for* **Lisa**.

Eleanor You witless little tart!

Brian No!

Brian *tries to stop* **Eleanor**. *Grabs her skirt, accidentally ripping if off to reveal bimbo underwear beneath.* **Brian** *hurls backwards, knocking* **Richard** *over just as* **Nick** *hurls a pie.* **Brian** *gets the pie.* **Nick** *throws another,* **Richard** *ducks and* **Lisa** *gets the pie.*

Nick Eighteen years I've known you. Eighteen sodding years!

Nick *breaks a bottle.*

Richard No!

Brian Oh, no.

Eleanor Nick. No.

Nick I'll cut your fucking heart out.

Eleanor Nick. No.

Eleanor *takes it from him.*

Nick Careful.

Eleanor I've got it.

Nick Don't cut yourself.

Eleanor I'm fine.

Nick I'm sorry.

Eleanor It's all right. Sit down now. Calm down. Richard, sit down. Nick's all right. He's not going to hurt anyone.

Richard *sits.*

Eleanor Are you all right?

Lisa Loose tooth.

Eleanor Leave it alone. The gum'll harden up.

Eleanor *hands* **Lisa** *some whisky.*

Lisa K'you.

Brian That's better. Let's try and keep a sense of proportion.

Eleanor Brian's right. It's important to keep things in perspective.

Brian Act with a bit of dignity.

Eleanor That's the word I was looking for.

She empties the trifle over **Richard**. *He wipes custard from his eyes.*

Richard What the hell are you wearing anyway?

Eleanor What, this? My little tribute to Benny. I was saving it for later. It was going to be just for you, but what the hell. What is it about her then? What's she got that I haven't? That can't be it, surely? Big tits? Blonde hair? Short fat hairy legs? It's not sex then? It's not all bodies you find repellent? Just mine? These particular breasts, these particular legs, this particular cunt?

Richard Don't, Ellie.

Eleanor Well then what?

Richard She's different, that's all.

Eleanor Oh I see. Different.

Lisa Ellie; you'll catch cold.

Eleanor Shut up, Sidney.

Richard Please, Ellie.

Eleanor Look at this though; whoever this is. I would have been this for you.

She sits. **Brian** *tears up his ticket to Amsterdam. The phone rings.*

Richard Yes? What (*Pause.*) Yes. Thanks, Toby. Bye.

Puts phone down.

Brian What now?

Richard He's dead, Brian.

Brian Les Rollins?

Richard No.

Brian Who then?

Richard Frankie Howerd.

Brian When?

Richard Tonight. They just found him.

Baby cries. After a while, **Lisa** *rises.*

Lisa It was his heart.

Exit **Lisa**.

Eleanor Never rains but it pours, does it? Nick? Want to come upstairs with me and be different? Anyone here want to fuck me then, or shall I put my dress back on? Richard. I want you and your bones out of here tonight.

Richard We'll discuss it later.

Eleanor We will not discuss it. If you want to leave, you will leave tonight.

Lisa *returns with the carrycot.*

Lisa Nick. Do you want to drive us home Nick, or shall I?

Nick *crosses and looks at the baby.*

Nick I'll drive.

Richard I don't think you should Nick; you're not sober.

Nick I'm fine.

Richard No, Nick. You can't drive.

Nick What fucking business is it of yours?

Eleanor Maybe he's right, Nick.

Nick I'm perfectly capable of driving *my* wife, and *my* child, safely home.

Lisa I'll drive. I haven't drunk much. It was just a silly thing. Ellie? Nick, it was just . . . Tell them.

Richard It was nothing.

Lisa And it was only . . .

Lisa Twice.

Richard Once.

Lisa Once.

Richard Twice. Once or twice.

Lisa And we were very careful. Weren't we? Tell him.

Richard We were careful.

Nick I don't want to know.

Lisa I want you to know. I want you to know we were careful, so the baby *is* y . . .

Nick Lisa! If it's finished, it's finished.

Lisa It is finished.

Richard It's finished.

Nick Then it's done with.

Lisa I just wanted you to know.

Nick I'll start her up.

Richard Need a push?

Nick If she needs a push I'll push her.

Exit **Nick**.

Lisa I've left his things upstairs.

Richard I'll get them.

Exit **Richard**.

Lisa Ellie . . .

Eleanor Who do you love?

Lisa What?

Eleanor It's a simple question. Who do you love?

Lisa Um. . . .

Eleanor Do you love anyone?

Lisa Well, if you must know. Graham Fisher.

Eleanor Who's he?

Lisa Man I met at work.

Eleanor You're screwing a man you met at work as well?

Lisa Ellie! What Graham and I share is beyond sex. Sex with Graham would be too real. You wouldn't understand.

Enter **Richard**.

Richard Here.

Lisa Thank you.

Enter **Nick**.

Nick Ready?

Lisa Yes.

Nick Put him in the car.

Lisa Come on then.

Nick I'll follow you.

Lisa Nick?

Nick Put him in the car.

Exit **Lisa**. **Nick** *goes to* **Richard** *and stands facing him. He clenches, unclenches his fists, then clamps* **Richard***'s head between spread hands. Almost as if he's going to kiss him. Bursts into tears. Embraces* **Richard***, then lets him go and takes time to recover.*

Nick Stay away from us.

Exit **Nick**.

Richard Can we talk in the morning?

Eleanor It's not his is it?

Richard I don't know.

Eleanor He knows.

Richard Ellie, it meant nothing.

Eleanor Nothing doesn't cry for its mother.

Richard I'm going to have a shower.

Eleanor I meant what I said.

Richard I'll sleep on the sofa.

Eleanor You'll sleep with me. Or you'll leave. Tonight.

Richard This is my home.

Eleanor Don't do this. Don't make it me. Don't make me make you do what you damn well know you want to.

Tries to take off her wedding ring.

Richard Where shall I go?

Eleanor You can stay at Brian's. Can he stay at yours?

Brian Oh, yes. He can stay at mine.

*Exit **Richard**. **Eleanor** tries to take off her ring. Looks at **Brian**'s Amsterdam ticket.*

Eleanor Do you want some sellotape for this?

Brian Oh, I'm not bothered. I don't think I could cope. I've got my little flat. I've got some good friends. And I enjoy a good laugh now and again; why spoil it? Things rarely turn out the way you expect, do they? And you sit there thinking; I should have seen this coming. And then you realise I did, I did see this coming. And I sent out invitations.

Eleanor My last ten years with him. He'll end up with some twenty-four-year-old, when he's ready. They'll have a cottage full of kids. And I'll have a couple of cats, a stall on Camden market and the odd holiday in Florence.

Brian Sounds utter bliss.

Eleanor I'll hang myself first. All the little taps inside me are turning themselves off.

Brian You don't really want him to go, do you?

*She looks up. Enter **Richard** with bag, a few things stuffed in.*

Richard I'm not sure this is the way we should do this.

Eleanor What is the way we should do this?

Richard There are better ways.

Eleanor I don't think so.

Brian We off then?

Richard Looks like it.

Brian *rises, gives* **Richard** *a key.* **Eleanor** *tries to get her wedding ring off.*

Brian Let yourself in. I'll come across when I've done some tidying up.

Eleanor That's all right, I'll do that.

Brian It won't take five minutes.

Exit **Brian**.

Richard Ellie.

Eleanor Go away.

Richard Listen.

Eleanor Don't touch me. Please don't.

Richard Are you sure this is what you want?

Eleanor You know what I want.

Richard You want me to go?

Eleanor I want a baby! I want a baby! I want a baby!

Eleanor *breaks down. Hurts her hand trying to get her ring off.*

Eleanor All right. Stay. Stay, all right?

Richard Well . . . I've packed now. I may as well . . .

Eleanor What?

Richard Go.

Eleanor I see.

Richard Bye.

Exit **Richard**. *The ring comes off quite easily.*

Brian I've put the kettle on.

Eleanor You don't have to stay; I'll be all right.

Brian Oh, I'd rather. Shouldn't be you sitting on your own.

Eleanor I'd better start practising.

Brian Look, if you want me to go I'll go. Now do you want me to go?

Eleanor No.

Brian I'll stay then.

Eleanor Thank you.

He sits. They hold hands.

Brian You smell nice.

Eleanor Four Seven Eleven.

Brian Oh, that's nice. She'd have liked that.

Eleanor Poor old Frankie.

Brian No, I didn't expect that. All of a sudden everyone's dying. And you never expect it. I watched mum die for two years, but I never expected it. Oh. I miss her so much.

Eleanor Oh, Brian.

Brian What we both need is a nice young man.

Eleanor A nice virile young man.

Brian A nice virile young man who's looking for love.

Eleanor Or in my case, for his mother.

Brian Could be the same chap then.

Eleanor You can have him after me.

Brian I wouldn't deprive you.

Eleanor I wouldn't want him for long. I babysat for them last week. He wouldn't go to sleep. I did something I was so ashamed of, but I couldn't not. I crept upstairs, took off my top, and let him suck. I can still feel his mouth.

She closes her eyes. **Brian** *smells her, then touches her breast.*

Eleanor Brian.

Brian Mmm?

Eleanor What are you doing?

Brian You're a very attractive woman, Ellie.

Eleanor You're a homosexual, Brian.

Brian I know.

Eleanor But thanks.

Brian Mum used to say I was always one to show willing.

Brian *begins to sing quietly: Frankie Howerd's 'Three Little Fishies'*.*

Eleanor *joins in. They sing until they're laughing too much to continue.*

Brian Well, you've got to see the funny side, haven't you?

The End

**Three Little Fishies* by Saxie Dowell. © Campbell Connelly & Co. Ltd.

METHUEN MODERN PLAYS

include work by

Jean Anouilh
John Arden
Margaretta D'Arcy
Peter Barnes
Brendan Behan
Edward Bond
Bertolt Brecht
Howard Brenton
Jim Cartwright
Caryl Churchill
Noël Coward
Sarah Daniels
Shelagh Delaney
David Edgar
Dario Fo
Michael Frayn
John Guare
Peter Handke
Terry Johnson
Kaufman & Hart
Barrie Keeffe
Larry Kramer
Stephen Lowe

Doug Lucie
John McGrath
David Mamet
Arthur Miller
Mtwa, Ngema & Simon
Tom Murphy
Peter Nichols
Joe Orton
Louise Page
Luigi Pirandello
Stephen Poliakoff
Franca Rame
David Rudkin
Willy Russell
Jean-Paul Sartre
Sam Shepard
Wole Soyinka
C. P. Taylor
Theatre Workshop
Sue Townsend
Timberlake Wertenbaker
Victoria Wood